Awesome Arizona

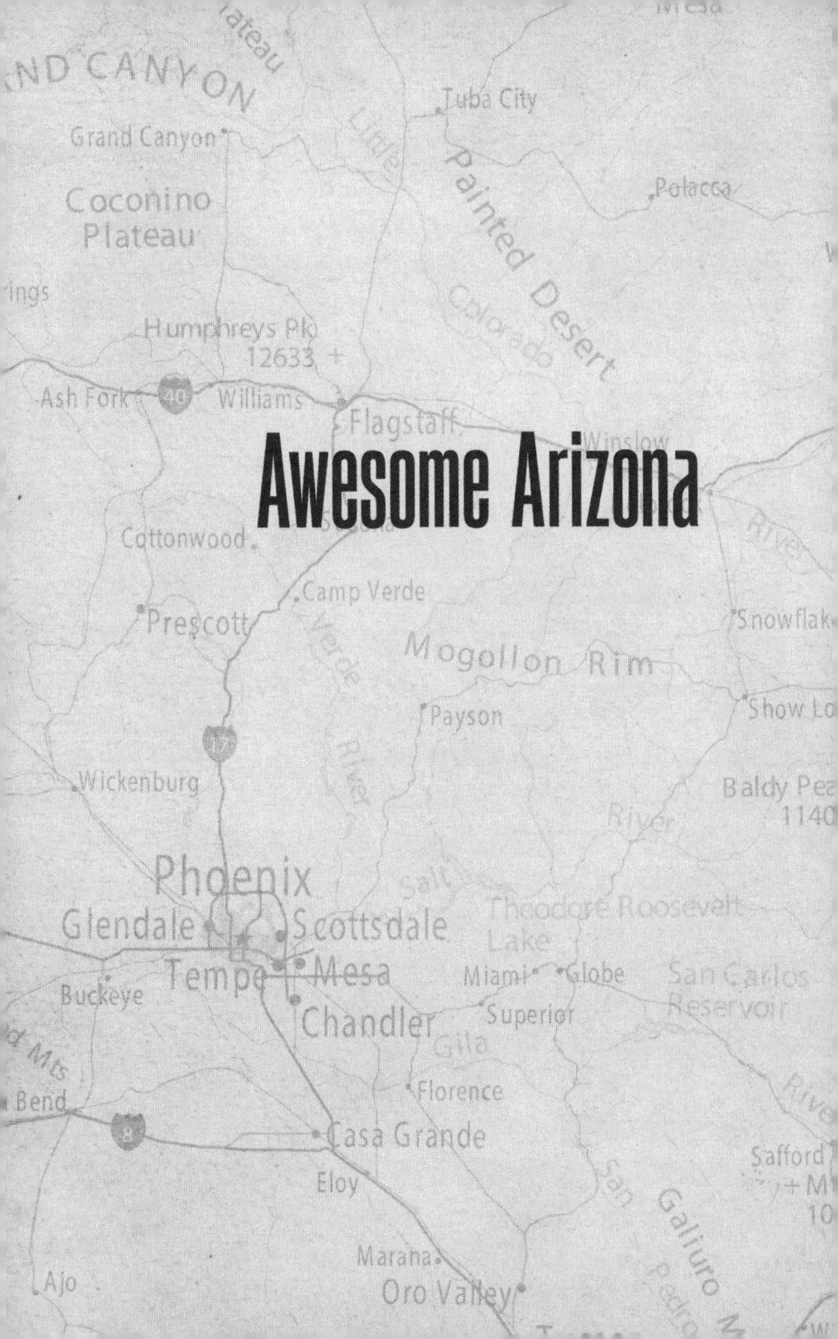

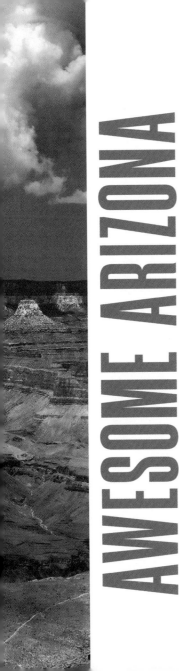

AWESOME ARIZONA

200 Amazing Facts about the Grand Canyon State

ROGER NAYLOR

University of New Mexico Press
Albuquerque

ISBN 978-0-8263-6457-9 (paper)
ISBN 978-0-8263-6458-6 (electronic)

Library of Congress Control Number: 2022947718

Founded in 1889, the University of New Mexico sits on the
traditional homelands of the Pueblo of Sandia. The original
peoples of New Mexico—Pueblo, Navajo, and Apache—
since time immemorial have deep connections to the land
and have made significant contributions to the broader
community statewide. We honor the land itself and those
who remain stewards of this land throughout the generations and also acknowledge our committed relationship to
Indigenous peoples. We gratefully recognize our history.

Cover photograph by Rick Mortensen
Designed by Felicia Cedillos
Composed in Utopia 8.75/14

To Dan, Michael, Rico, and Steve—
the rest of the Acme Comedy Company.
Thanks for the laughs, amigos!

Acknowledgments

The author wishes to express his gratitude to several people. Thanks to Jill Cassidy for the endless opportunities she has afforded me to explore this state and for her wise and gentle guidance. Thanks to Rick Mortensen for his wonderful photos and support. I'm grateful to Ken Lapides for his skill and keen eye. And a very special thanks to Mike Koopsen for his remarkable photos, his enthusiasm, and friendship. It's always a pleasure when we get to work together. Also, I am very appreciative of the many folks I encounter and work with across the state, and occasionally badger with questions—Chamber of Commerce members, tourism boards, visitor center staffers and volunteers, park rangers, and business owners. Thanks for your hard work and patience with me.

Most importantly, I owe this sweet Arizona life to my beautiful and talented wife, Michele. She makes it all possible, and every day is a joy because I get to wake up next to her.

Welcome to the absolutely, utterly awesome 48th state. Photo by the author.

INTRODUCTION

Look, it just felt like someone needed to come out and say it. Arizona is awesome!

I realized that right away—soon as I showed up in Flagstaff, an eager college student, astounded by the drama of the mountainous landscape. It proved to be love at first sight for me, a romance for the ages. My swoony admiration for the state quickly derailed my college aspirations. I made the dean's list my first semester, but by the second semester I was on academic probation. Because by then I had come to realize that I could get up in the morning, grab my books, and hurry to class . . . or I could hitchhike to the Grand Canyon.

Or to the red rock country of Sedona. Or to the lean, sun-gnawed desert filled with stately saguaros. Or to the high slopes of the San Francisco Peaks forested with ponderosa pines that smelled of butterscotch, and white-barked aspen trees growing in clustered bunches like a ghostly choir, their leaves clattering soft in the breeze, sounding like butterfly applause. Right from the start, Arizona taught me what's truly important in life—to play hooky every chance you get.

So take it from me, Arizona is rugged and gorgeous and historic and weird and funny and utterly magnificent. It's full of surprises, not what most people expect at all. Certainly every state can make similar claims; no one's arguing that. But with this book I'm piling up the evidence.

Start with the size. Arizona is vast, the sixth-largest state in the union,

Tall saguaros are the defining feature of Arizona's Sonoran Desert. Photo by the author.

an epic landscape bulging with mountains, slashed by canyons, and blown apart by volcanoes. The world's largest ponderosa pine forest spreads across the north, and the south bristles with an arsenal of the country's tallest cacti. We have sandy beaches and alpine tundra, meteor-gouged craters and towering waterfalls. We have every life zone found between Mexico and Canada.

Jaguars leave tropical jungles to pad softly through our southern mountains. Wolves howl at our moon, and the deadliest scorpion in North America hides under our rocks like an unsheathed blade. We have more kinds of rattlesnakes than anywhere else and the only venomous

A snowstorm turns the South Rim of the Grand Canyon into a winter wonderland. Courtesy of Mike Koopsen, Sedona.

lizard in the country. Now who's ready for a hike? You better be, because our trails are the stuff of legend.

Trees that once shaded dinosaurs are still here. Our hunters brought down mammoths, and our gunslingers shot their way into the history books. We saved the unicorn. We saved Route 66. We invented the chimichanga.

Arizona is the Dwarf Car Capital of the world, and we have the only nuke with a gift shop. The world's largest antique is a major tourist attraction, and the booze flows like water in the nation's second-smallest bar. You'll find 22 sovereign nations in Arizona and more national monuments than anywhere else. We rock out on the world's largest pipe organ. You can't get to the moon without going through Arizona, which just happens to be the sunniest place on earth. You might encounter Bigfoot or spot

Working cowboys are a long-standing Arizona tradition. Courtesy of Mike Koopsen, Sedona.

a UFO. You can definitely take a selfie with the world's largest kokopelli, kachina doll, and rosebush.

You can swim and snow-ski in the same day in Arizona. You can go to college to become a cowboy. Despite it being an arid state, the largest and second-largest man-made lakes are here, and we have waterfalls taller than Niagara Falls. We keep the nation healthy all winter long with salads, and then, just when it is needed most, start waving around bacon-wrapped hot dogs from the borderlands. You're welcome.

Here's another fact I've learned about Arizona—it invokes a fierce pride in residents. That respect flows from the Indigenous people who hold the land sacred and have been living in harmony with it for millennia. That gives us all something to strive for.

Arizona-born residents can often trace their roots back for generations and delight in sharing stories about their favorite relatives who worked as a lawman or became a notorious horse thief.

Of course, Arizona is often regarded as nothing but a land of transplants. The common perception is that this state shelters an unconnected population with few common interests, people that are still loyal

Poppies carpet the desert following wet winters. Photo by the author.

to previous homesteads. But I've found just the opposite to be true. Sure, some folks landed here because of happenstance. Yet plenty, like me, are here for reasons of our own, and our passion and pride in Arizona knows no bounds.

We're here because golden poppies blaze across the desert floor in spring like a satin fire. We're here because skies are relentlessly blue—not gray or gloomy or soggy—but sharp as cut glass while still violet-soft. We're here because our trails are winding, our horizons are shoved wide, and the outdoors laps at our doorsteps. We're here because horses run free along the Salt River and wild burros rule Oatman and neon still shimmers along Route 66. We're here because mountains heal and the desert seduces. We're here for the burritos and date shakes and history and hummingbirds and swinging-door saloons and the Grand Canyon and Sedona and Monument Valley and ferocious heat and pristine snow

A soft golden sunset settles over the Grand Canyon. Courtesy of Mike Koopsen, Sedona.

and fragrant forests and the glorious, lavish, dramatic sunsets. We're here because it feels good to dance in the rain, because we can see the Milky Way from our porches, and because we can hike every single day of the year.

If the Garden of Eden had a liquor license and served really good tacos, they would have called it Arizona. This is paradise.

I knew this was where I belonged when Arizona stole my breath, squeezed my heart, and opened my eyes all those decades ago. I'm here because happiness doesn't exist for me anywhere else. Hey, it's all in the book. If it doesn't convince you, don't worry. I'm already rambling around my big old yard working on the next book. It's not like I'll ever run out of things to write about in awesome Arizona.

Now that's a fact.

1. Arizona is the sunniest state in the nation.

Florida calls itself the Sunshine State, but that's only because they're playing fast and loose with the truth. Arizona is actually the sunniest state. It's not even close. We bathe in the stuff. Wash away our cares and cleanse our souls with the stuff.

No place understands sunshine like Yuma. Tucked away in the southwestern corner of the state, Yuma perches on the bank of the Colorado River surrounded by farm fields and date groves. Skies are deep blue and cloudless because Yuma also happens to be the sunniest place, period. Not just in Arizona, not just in the United States, but on *earth*! In Yuma, the sun shines more than 90 percent of all daylight hours. That translates to more than 4,000 hours each year of sweet vitamin D.

As for the second-sunniest city in the world, look no further than Phoenix. There's a reason the Phoenix metropolitan area is called the Valley of the Sun. The big city basks in sunshine 85 percent of the time. Tucson, which sits at a slightly higher elevation than Phoenix and is just a bit cooler and wetter, turns out to be the sixth-sunniest city on the planet. Statistics come from the World Meteorological Association, based on their sunshine averages over a period of nearly 30 years. (Other US cities with a high rate of sunshine are Las Vegas at number four and El Paso at number ten. All the rest are in Africa.)

As for Florida, which doesn't have a single city in the top ten rankings, let them keep their little motto. Grand Canyon State sounds catchier anyway.

2. Arizona is the only state that contains one of the Seven Natural Wonders of the World.

Grand Canyon is 277 miles long, a mile deep, and up to 18 miles wide. Yet it still manages to leap out and startle you.

Unlike aboveground features, you don't glimpse it off in the distance and watch it grow large and magnificent the closer you get. You don't see the canyon at all on your approach. Not until you emerge from the forest and stand right there on the rim as the world falls away at your feet and the eyeballs spin in your head like they do in old-time cartoons and your heart suddenly pounds a terrifying drumbeat against your chest. Gazing down into the abyss, it feels like you're peeking at God's diary.

Nothing prepares you for the size or scale or rawness or the intensity of the colors or the haunting of the haze that trails away at the edge of your vision. Nothing prepares you for the complexity of the patterns, those sloping terraces of temples and thrones, castles and domes that spill endlessly downward into ancient depths and seem to look different from season to season and hour to hour. How can it all change so fast? Cliffs blush pale one minute then rage and scowl the next. Nothing in nature is as moody as the Grand Canyon.

When the canyon trembles, you quickly step back. It takes a moment to realize that it was only a trick of the sunlight. The broad mosaic of shadows and light that shift across the gulf instills a sense of animation to the landscape. Beneath the stillness is movement. Beneath the calm is the echo of violence, the grinding of tectonic plates, the relentless chisel of a river, the soft knife of the eons. Listen carefully while you're here because silence is louder at the Grand Canyon than anywhere else.

This erosional masterpiece, from one end to the other, lies entirely within Arizona's borders. Grand Canyon was designated as a national

Nothing in nature is as moody as Grand Canyon. Courtesy of Mike Koopsen, Sedona.

park in 1919. It receives over 6 million visitors annually, making it the second most popular of the nation's parks most years, behind only Great Smoky Mountains National Park.

Arizona's Big Ditch keeps good company. According to the *World Atlas*, the other six Natural Wonders of the World are Mount Everest, the Great Barrier Reef, the Harbor of Rio de Janeiro, Victoria Falls, the Northern Lights, and Paricutin, a volcano in Mexico.

3. Jaguars still prowl our canyons and mountains.

Sleek, savage, and immensely powerful, jaguars can be found in Latin

American jungles, the Amazon rain forest, and the rugged mountains of southeastern Arizona. At least seven male jaguars have been seen in Arizona since 1996.

What an amazing sight to witness the elegant felines slipping through the Arizona timber on cushioned paws! Jaguars are the third-biggest cat in the world—behind only tigers and lions. They stalk and attack from ambush but, instead of going for the throat, bite through the skull with powerful jaws, their teeth piercing the brain of their prey.

While once prominent in the Southwest, jaguars were thought to have been eliminated from the United States decades ago. The last recorded female jaguar in the United States was shot dead in Arizona in 1963. Yet in 1996 two different male jaguars were photographed roaming Arizona's lonely southern mountains. Others have followed.

The endangered animals face threats from both sides of the border. Poaching, habitat degradation, and a border wall cutting off migratory corridors all put added pressure on the jaguar's survival as a species. Yet despite the obstacles, the big cats still hunt in the Arizona hills. Studies show that there is expansive habitat to reclaim on this side of the border, if the jaguars can just reach it.

There have also been several sightings in Arizona of ocelots, a strikingly beautiful medium-sized cat. The state represents the northernmost range of both predators.

4. If you eat a salad in the winter, it was grown in Arizona.

All those hours of sunshine are put to good use. Yuma produces more than 90 percent of the nation's leafy vegetables consumed in this country from November to March. Yuma is home to nine salad plants that produce bagged lettuce and salad mixes. During peak production, each

The fertile green fields of Yuma keep the nation fed during the winter months. Photo by the author.

plant processes more than 2 million pounds of lettuce per day.

Yuma farmers benefit from soil enriched by sediments deposited by the Colorado River over millions of years, technological advancements in irrigation, and a strong, skilled labor force. More than 175 crops are grown in Yuma year-round.

With more and more people wanting to know the origin of their food, the Yuma Visitors Bureau created the Field to Feast tours in 2011 in partnership with the University of Arizona Cooperative Extension.

Field to Feast tours gives participants a chance to harvest fresh produce and eat a meal created from it just a couple of hours later. In between the field and the feast, visitors get a peek behind the scenes of Yuma's multibillion dollar agricultural industry. Field to Feast tour dates run January through February. (800) 293-0071, www.visityuma.com.

5. You can light a candle at America's only Catholic shrine to a sinner.

In a quiet alcove in Tucson, people come to mourn loss and love. They come to rid themselves of their own sorrow. The primary legend surrounding El Tiradito in Barrio Viejo is a steamy one. It involves a tragic love triangle in the 1870s. A young sheepherder named Juan Oliveras began an affair with the mother of his young bride. I know, right? When caught in the act, Juan was chased into the dusty street and axed to death by the woman's husband, his father-in-law.

Due to the nature of his sin, the dead man could not be buried in consecrated ground. He was planted where he fell, and the shrine sprang up honoring the memory of El Tiradito, "the little castaway."

Located south of downtown Tucson, Barrio Viejo is known for its brightly colored adobe homes and authentic Mexican eateries. It is a neighborhood teeming with character, yet it might very well have been wiped off the map if not for the mysterious power of the shrine.

In the 1960s and '70s big swaths of the barrio had already been bull-dozed as part of an urban development push. Some 80 acres were lost just in the construction of the Tucson Convention Center. When a freeway was proposed that would have destroyed the rest of the neighborhood, locals rallied. They fought to get the El Tiradito shrine listed on the National Register of Historic Places. When they succeeded in 1971, the highway plan collapsed. Today, a revitalized Barrio Viejo contains one of the largest collections of 19th-century adobe buildings in the United States.

Visitors come to the small grotto to light candles and leave offerings. Often they will scribble their own hopes and prayers on little pieces of paper and tuck them into the cracks of the weathered adobe wall. Legend has it that if a candle burns through the night, your wish will come true. That's how El Tiradito also became known as the Wishing Shrine.

6. Arizona has more national monuments than any other state.

With the Grand Canyon, we have an iconic national park. Our other national parks include Petrified Forest and Saguaro. A notch below national park designation, which requires an act of Congress, are the

A hiker explores the depths of Paria Canyon in the Vermilion Cliffs National Monument. Courtesy of Mike Koopsen, Sedona.

national monuments. Those are also places of remarkable beauty and/or history and can be created by a presidential decree. Arizona contains 18 national monuments, more than any other state, and they protect spectacular scenery and cultural treasures.

Arizona's national monuments are:

Agua Fria National Monument
Canyon de Chelly National Monument
Casa Grande Ruins National Monument
Chiricahua National Monument
Grand Canyon–Parashant National Monument
Hohokam Pima National Monument
Ironwood Forest National Monument
Montezuma Castle National Monument
Navajo National Monument

Organ Pipe Cactus National Monument
Pipe Spring National Monument
Sonoran Desert National Monument
Sunset Crater Volcano National Monument
Tonto National Monument
Tuzigoot National Monument
Vermilion Cliffs National Monument
Walnut Canyon National Monument
Wupatki National Monument

7. The world's largest contiguous ponderosa pine forest spreads across Arizona.

We're so much more than just desert. A massive pine forest stretches from Williams and Flagstaff crossing the top of the Mogollon Rim and running through the White Mountains to the New Mexico border like an ocean of green. Ponderosa pines are among the tallest trees in the Southwest, growing to heights over 200 feet with huge trunks 3–4 feet across. They are found primarily at elevations between 6,000 and 8,000 feet. The mild, wet winters and pattern of rain and dry spells make the Arizona high country a prime habitat for the tall, regal trees.

8. Also, our forests smell faintly of butterscotch.

It's not because Keebler elves are toiling away on their tree cookies, which has to violate all sorts of health codes. It's actually the trees emitting the soft perfume of butterscotch (some say vanilla). Stick your nose in the folds of the bark of a ponderosa pine, and you catch the distinctive whiff of vanilla (some say butterscotch). At times the air is ripe with the haunting incense, a welcome companion on any summer hike.

9. Arizona has more mountains than any of the other Mountain States.

Again, we're not just desert. Sorry, Colorado, Idaho, Montana, Nevada, New Mexico, Utah, and Wyoming. Arizona is rugged and mountainous and snowy and surprisingly vertical. We have 3,928 mountain summits and peaks poking holes in our azure skies. That's a lot of high country spread all across the state. There are at least 26 peaks that top out above 10,000 feet.

The Chiricahua Mountains rise over the deserts of southeastern Arizona, one of the many mountain ranges covering the state. Photo by the author.

10. Arizona is the only state to contain all four major American deserts.

OK, so we're not all desert but we keep plenty of it on hand. Of course, the Sonoran Desert is our signature landscape and is the most biologically diverse desert. It's hard to call any desert lush, but the Sonoran qualifies. With its pattern of summer monsoons and winter rains, the Sonoran Desert is the wettest desert in the world. It bristles with plant life, which in turn increases animal life. The tall cactus desert is a thriving habitat that is surprisingly seductive and features an array of distinct mountain ranges separated by wide valleys and forests of elegant saguaros. Hot in the summer, which should come as no surprise, it is also America's warmest—deliciously warm—winter desert.

Along with the Sonoran, you'll also find the Mojave, Chihuahuan, and Great Basin Deserts (although some experts disagree about the latter). Arizona is the only state that can claim elements of all four.

11. The best-preserved meteor crater in the world is gouged from the landscape just outside of Winslow.

Imagine a peaceful day some 50,000 years ago. Earth spins on its axis, minding its own beeswax. All of a sudden, POW! Out of nowhere, it gets hit with a continent-rattling shot to the high plains of what would become northern Arizona. Meteors are sucker punches from the universe.

As mammoths and giant ground sloths grazed the grasslands, a slab of iron and nickel 150 feet across screamed through the skies. It struck with an explosive force greater than 20 million tons of TNT. The impact gouged out a giant bowl-shaped cavity 700 feet deep and over 4,000 feet across, excavating several hundred million tons of rock and dirt. Kaboom, baby!

This is the first proven and best-preserved impact meteor crater on the planet. There's been some slight erosion and the bottom has partly filled in, but essentially the big hole hasn't changed much in 50,000 years. Visitors can enjoy comfortable facilities, including an interactive museum and a movie with lots of explosive graphics. Paved walking trails skirt the rim and lead to several prime viewing platforms. (928) 289-5898, www.meteorcrater.com.

12. The US Postal Service (USPS) delivers mail by mule to only one location, and that's in Arizona.

In the age of drones, instant delivery, and overnight shipping, one place still takes it on the hoof. USPS mules carry mail, food, and supplies down an 8-mile trail to the Havasupai people, an American Indian tribe who lives in the village of Supai, deep in the Grand Canyon. It is known as the most remote community in the lower 48 states.

The Havasupai have resided within the canyon for more than 1,000 years and are known as the "people of the blue-green water." They are the guardians of an exotic corner of the canyon that seems like a tropical island paradise featuring a series of cascading turquoise waterfalls spilling down red cliffs.

Mules also deliver the mail to Phantom Ranch along the Colorado River in Grand Canyon National Park, but those chores are handled by Xanterra, a park concessionaire. If you happen to be spending the night

The Havasupai Indian Reservation includes the remote village of Supai, and a series of spectacular waterfalls spilling into turquoise pools. Courtesy of Mike Koopsen, Sedona.

at Phantom, you can send a postcard or letter to the surface world. It will get stamped: "Mailed by Mule at the Bottom of the Grand Canyon—Phantom Ranch." Pretty cool, right?

13. Phoenix Zoo saved the unicorn.

The Arabian oryx is an almost pure-white antelope, with dark legs and a blaze of black across the face. Both males and females have long slender curved horns, perfectly aligned. It is believed that these elegant creatures gave rise to the legend of the unicorn. Hunted for food and for the presumed magical power of its horns, the Arabian oryx went extinct in the wild in 1972.

Fortunately, the Phoenix Zoo and the Fauna and Flora International (FFI) were already on the case. In 1962, the FFI began rounding up a handful of Arabian oryx and transported them to Arizona. The newly opened Phoenix Zoo became keeper of the "World Herd." The plan was to establish a breeding program and reintroduce offspring back into the wild.

"Operation Oryx" proved to be a resounding success, and in 1981 the animals were reintroduced on the Arabian Peninsula. In 2011 the International Union for the Conservation of Nature changed the status of the Arabian oryx from endangered to vulnerable. It marked the first time a species has been reclassified as vulnerable after it had been listed as extinct in the wild.

Founded in 1962 by Robert Maytag of the Maytag appliance family, the Phoenix Zoo was geared toward conservation from the beginning. It is one of the largest privately owned nonprofit zoos in the United States with more than 3,000 animals on display and 2.5 miles of walking trails. It also includes a conservation center continuing their work in breeding and raising threatened animals for release into the wild. (602) 286-3800, www.phoenixzoo.org.

14. We grow the largest cactus in the United States.

We may be the Grand Canyon State, but the saguaro cactus serves as our iconic symbol. The tall columnar cactus is a defining plant of the Sonoran Desert, adding fine vertical notes to the lowlands and marching up rocky slopes. Saguaros commonly reach heights of 40 feet, although the tallest ever measured towered 78 feet into the air. Some develop dozens of arms as they age, while others remain a straight spiny pole. No one knows why.

Yet they seem in no hurry to rise up. Most saguaros start out sheltered beneath the branches of a "nurse plant." That protective environment is needed because the tender cacti are extremely slow growers. It can take 10 years before a saguaro is much more than an inch tall. They pick up the pace a little after that but never experience any kind of hormone-fueled teenage growth spurt. They won't begin to produce arms until they're 50 to 70 years old.

At 125 years, a saguaro is generally considered an adult. They can live for two full centuries, maybe longer. There's still plenty about these lean giants—these redwoods of the desert—that scientists don't know, like why some saguaros produce a fanlike form atop the trunk or at the end of an arm.

But those cristate or "crested" saguaros are extremely rare. Much more common are the tall stately saguaros we recognize from cowboy movies and sunset photographs: saguaros spearing the clouds with upraised arms. They are the personification of elegance . . . at least at first glance. Look deeper and their personality emerges. You begin to appreciate their whimsical spirit. Using only their arms, saguaros do impersonations and act out scenes all over the desert: sweethearts smooching, a hitchhiker, a prophet, a personal trainer offering encouragement, gunfighters about to draw down, even a dance-off. It's no surprise.

Spend a hundred years in the desert and see if you don't develop a sense of humor.

Saguaros are the guardians of the Sonoran Desert! But instead of an exclamation point at the end of that sentence, imagine a saguaro. Saguaros are the exclamation points of Arizona.

15. We played the longest poker game in history.

It took place at the Bird Cage Theatre in Tombstone and ran for more than 8 years.

The O.K. Corral may have the name recognition in Tombstone, but at the other end of Allen Street sits another legend of the Wild West. The Bird Cage Theatre also racked up a significantly higher body count than the corral. The combination theater, saloon, gambling hall, and brothel (now that's one-stop shopping for cowboys) opened in 1881—and stayed open 24 hours a day, 365 days a year. The *New York Times* once called the joint "the roughest, bawdiest, most wicked night spot between Basin Street and the Barbary Coast." At least 26 people are thought to have died on the floor of the Bird Cage, and not a heart attack among them.

Downstairs housed the poker room. Despite the $1,000 buy-in, the action ran continuously for 8 years, 5 months, and 3 days, making it the world's longest poker game in history. Plenty of famous names handled the pasteboards during the marathon session, including Bat Masterson, Diamond Jim Brady, Adolph Busch, George Randolph Hearst, and John Henry "Doc" Holliday.

The Bird Cage closed in 1889 as the mines were shutting down. The

The Bird Cage Theatre is a well-preserved time capsule full of bullet holes and ghosts. Photo by the author.

building was sealed up and left undisturbed, so almost everything on display is original. Today it serves as an intriguing museum. Wander through while studying the dusty artifacts and sticking fingers in some of the 140-plus bullet holes that aerate the building. The Bird Cage is said to be one of the most haunted buildings in Arizona. They offer nightly ghost tours so you can see for yourself. 535 E. Allen St., (520) 457-3421, www.tombstonebirdcage.com.

16. Our rodeos are absolutely historic.

In Prescott, the World's Oldest Rodeo dates back to 1888 and sprawls across the Fourth of July weekend (and then some) every year. This is the Super Bowl for the bowlegged. What began as a chance for local cowboys to show off their ranch-honed skills has grown into a weeklong celebration. One of Arizona's largest parades kicks things off, and spectators can cheer on contests like bronc riding, bull riding, barrel racing, and calf roping. Plenty of other activities take place outside the arena, including concerts, dances, and arts and crafts shows. www.worldsoldestrodeo.com.

One record-setting rodeo isn't enough for Arizona. In August, the World's Oldest Continuous Rodeo takes place in the pine forests of Payson. The story goes that Payson's event dates back to 1884, 4 years earlier than Prescott's. But detractors claim it was unorganized and not an official rodeo. When the Prescott rodeo went on hiatus during World War II, Payson seized the new title. And cowpokes have been showing up ever since. www.paysonprorodeo.com.

Since the Tucson Rodeo didn't start until 1925, it's not quite as historic. Yet it still managed to stake out its own claim to fame. The La Fiesta de los Vaqueros (Celebration of Cowboys) takes place in February and has continued to grow until it is one of the top 25 rodeos in North America. But the real showstopper is the parade that kicks off the festivities. The Tucson Rodeo Parade is the longest nonmotorized parade in the nation. It's 2.5 miles of feet, hooves, and wheels filled with Native American performers, marching bands, mariachis, historic wagons and floats, and plenty of cowboys. Even Tucson schools close for a couple of days to make sure kids have a chance to participate or attend. www.tucsonrodeo.com.

17. Only Arizona can claim the geological belligerence of the Mogollon Rim.

In a state that includes the Grand Canyon, Monument Valley, and the red rocks of Sedona, the great stone barrier of the Mogollon Rim rising 2,000 feet in a fierce vertical thrust from the desert floor to high pine forests may be Arizona's most startling feature.

The Mogollon Rim is a 200-mile-long escarpment, the result of geologic faulting. It slashes diagonally across Arizona from near the New Mexico border deep into Yavapai County. This great humped spine defines the southern edge of the Colorado Plateau, with ponderosa pine forests stretching across the upper plateaus and spilling down the slopes.

The rim was named for Juan Ignacio Flores Mogollon, the Spanish colonial governor of New Mexico, who served from 1712 to 1715. (There are some who believe it was named for the Spanish word for "mistletoe," a parasitic plant in the area, but that feels like a stretch to me.) This is also one of the key words that every Arizonan needs to know how to pronounce. It's "Muggy-own." Although you can also say "Muggy-yawn" if you want to sound continental.

The high cliffs of the Mogollon Rim exhibit the same layers of limestone and sandstone that are on display at the Grand Canyon. We see the same fine bone structure, the erosion-gnawed drama shared between our two biggest landforms. Some of Arizona's most spectacular canyons are cut from this towering wall, including Sycamore, Oak Creek, Wet Beaver, and West Clear Creek. When it comes to transition zones, none are more abrupt than the rim standing with its feet in desert and head in the clouds.

The views from atop the rim feel different than summit views. It's not just that you're above the landscape like on a mountain peak. You're also at the brink of something vast, teetering on a shoreline of sky and space. These are edge-of-the-world views. Waves of soft hills roll off into the distance, thousands of feet below. Meanwhile, you're alone with a vast slice of sky. The Mogollon Rim feels like heaven's porch.

18. Arizona has its very own Bigfoot.

The Mogollon Monster carries on the proud tradition of giant Sasquatch creatures roaming the woodlands all over the world. But this is no Johnny-come-lately to the Yeti brotherhood. The reclusive creature, said to stand over 7 feet tall, was reported all the way back in a 1903 edition of the *Arizona Republican* in which I. W. Stevens encountered the hirsute humanoid near the Grand Canyon. He discovered it drinking the blood of two young cougars it had killed.

Since that time, sightings of the apelike beast have been consistent. It is most often described as being covered in long black or reddish-brown hair, with a funky and pungent body odor. Sightings are most common in the forests of the Mogollon Rim.

19. McDonald's opened their very first drive-thru in Sierra Vista.

Arizona helped revolutionize the fast-food industry in 1975. That's when the McDonald's in Sierra Vista opened the company's very first drive-thru window. At the time soldiers from Fort Huachuca were not allowed to get out of their vehicles off-post while wearing fatigues. The owner of the McDonald's franchise near the base pushed out a bit of one wall and installed a sliding-glass window. Lines of hungry soldiers stretched around the building, and Big Macs flew out the window as fast as the crew could make them. For good or ill, our eating habits were forever altered—and the phrase "Please pull up to the window" entered the lexicon.

20. Arizona has the largest percentage of land designated as Native American lands among the 50 States.

More than one-fourth of the state is reservation land. Twenty-two distinct tribes make their homes in diverse settings that range from saguaro-clad desert to the river-carved depths of the Grand Canyon to the sandstone wonderland of the Colorado Plateau. Such stunning terrain harbors an array of scenic and cultural wonders.

In Arizona, 22 distinct American Indian communities preserve their culture and traditions on land that accounts for one-quarter of the state. Courtesy of Mike Koopsen, Sedona.

Please be respectful. Remember that each reservation possesses tribal sovereignty with its own government, laws, and rules for visitors. Many sacred areas are restricted and not open to non-tribal members. Alcohol is prohibited on tribal land except in designated areas like casinos.

The federally recognized tribes in Arizona are:

Ak-Chin Indian Community

Cocopah Indian Tribe

Colorado River Indian Tribes

Fort McDowell Yavapai Nation

Fort Mojave Indian Tribe

Fort Yuma Quechan Tribe

Gila River Indian Community

Havasupai Tribe

Hopi Tribe

Hualapai Tribe

Kaibab Band of Paiute Indians

Navajo Nation

Pascua Yaqui Tribe

Pueblo of Zuni

Salt River Pima-Maricopa Indian
Community

San Carlos Apache Tribe

San Juan Southern Paiute Tribe

Tohono O'odham Nation

Tonto Apache Tribe

White Mountain Apache Tribe

Yavapai-Apache Nation

Yavapai-Prescott Indian Tribe

21. Before GPS had satellites, it used Arizona.

Beyond the military applications, global positioning system (GPS) technology permeates our lives. Millions of civilian consumers use it as a navigational aid. It gives our phones superpowers, guides us to new restaurants, keeps hikers from getting lost on a trail, and turns us all into potential explorers. Pet owners use it to track their furry friends, and it's the centerpiece of a treasure-hunting game called geocaching. GPS functions today because of a constellation of satellites orbiting the earth more than 12,000 miles away in space. But before all that, it was operated by people booming around in big trucks across the lowest part of the Arizona desert.

GPS exists because of the work done at Yuma Proving Ground (YPG), a massive training area and military installation north of Yuma. The US Air Force created the GPS program, and developed and tested it at Yuma Proving Ground from 1974 through 1990.

A precision laser tracking system developed by Yuma engineers and specialized computer software designed at the proving ground (on room-sized 1960s vintage IBMs) provided data in real time. Before satellites, ground tests had to be conducted from modified two-and-a-half ton trucks. Aircraft were outfitted with antennas on their underside to pick up signals from ground receivers.

It's not surprising that Yuma Proving Ground would take the lead in such an important project. It is a virtually unparalleled laboratory. YPG covers 1,300 square miles in a landscape free from urban encroachment with extremely consistent weather patterns—350 sunny days and less than 3 inches of rainfall annually. Sparse vegetation limits many environmental concerns. Sea-level altitude makes it perfect for a helicopter test center.

The Apache helicopter, M-1 Abrams tank, Bradley Fighting Vehicle, Stryker armored vehicle, and virtually all of the US Army's artillery and ground weapon systems were tested here. YPG also contains the Western world's largest and most advanced mine, countermine, and demolitions test facility. Their work on unmanned aerial systems, commonly known as drones, dates back to the late 1950s.

22. The largest travertine natural bridge in the world is an Arizona state park.

Tucked away in a narrow valley between Pine and Payson, Tonto Natural Bridge stretches across a small stuttering creek. The span is 400 feet long and 183 feet high, forming an impressive tunnel. It was in the craggy darkness that prospector David Gowan hid from hostile Apaches in 1877. Impressed with the scenery when he finally emerged, the Scotsman settled in the valley and later convinced family members to join him. The bridge stayed in private hands until it became a state park in 1990. A historic lodge has been restored, and several short but steep hiking trails lead down to the bottom of the natural bridge and the creek. (928) 476-4202, www.azstateparks.com.

23. Arizona had its own version of Lady Godiva.

Except it was a dude. Climax Jim began garnering headlines in the 1890s with his exploits in the Arizona Territory. It began with his propensity to

From the creek, a lone hiker admires the immensity of Tonto Natural Bridge. Courtesy of Mike Koopsen, Sedona.

rustle any critter with four legs, but his legend grew thanks to his numerous escapes. Jim once claimed that he had escaped from every jail in Arizona except the Territorial Prison in Yuma, and it's not much of an exaggeration.

His real name was Rufus Nephew, and by all accounts he was a very likable fellow, with long, flowing hair and soulful eyes. He acquired his colorful nickname for his liberal use of Climax Chewing Tobacco.

Jim was arrested for the first time in 1894 for selling stolen cows to a slaughterhouse in Winslow. He was tossed into the Winslow jail but tunneled out the very first night by using a hidden pocketknife. He was 17.

A few months later, he was arrested for stealing a horse. The sheriff transporting Jim chained him to a post when they made camp. By daylight, the outlaw was long gone, leaving behind a busted chain link. This would be a pattern through Climax Jim's career. He was never hard to catch but holding on to him proved much trickier.

He dug his way out of the Globe jail with a spoon. He slithered out of leg shackles and climbed over the wall of the Solomonville jail. Picked the lock on the cell door at the jail in St. Johns and escaped. Once a hapless lawman was escorting Jim to the hoosegow, and they bedded down for camp handcuffed together. The next morning, the officer woke to find he was wearing the bracelets on both his wrists and was shy one prisoner.

Climax Jim's most famous escape came at the Springerville jail. There are different versions of the story, but the most beloved is that jailers felt Jim was overdue for a bath. They gave him a bar of soap and pointed him toward a horse trough. Instead, Jim—despite being stark and utterly naked without even spurs to jingle—jumped on a nearby horse and galloped through town with his long hair whipping in the wind, and escaped into the mountains.

Climax Jim finally left his wild ways behind him. He moved to San Diego and got a job digging wells. Alas, he should have stuck to rustling. In 1921, scaffolding gave way beneath him, and he fell to his death. What a pity he didn't have one more escape in him.

24. Arizona has the highest southernmost mountains in the continental United States.

Soaring to an elevation of 12,633 feet, Humphreys Peak is the highest point in Arizona. Humphreys is the tallest of a group of dormant volcanic summits known as the San Francisco Peaks that rise above Flagstaff. At the highest reaches, the slopes are cloaked in alpine tundra—the only example of tundra found in the state.

Humphreys and neighboring Agassiz Peak, which is 12,360 feet, are the

The San Francisco Peaks are the tallest mountains in Arizona, and the highest southernmost mountains in the continental United States. Courtesy of Mike Koopsen, Sedona.

southernmost peaks in the continental United States that top 12,000 feet above sea level.

For hardy souls, a hiking trail leaves from the Arizona Snowbowl (the ski resort) and snakes its way through the forest. It switchbacks up above the tree line, finally traversing the stark ridge of wind-scoured tundra to the summit of Humphreys Peak, the roof of Arizona.

25. Pluto was discovered from atop a hill overlooking downtown Flagstaff.

Clyde Tombaugh spotted the distant orb from Lowell Observatory in 1930, and for decades it held down the spot as the ninth planet of our solar system. Pluto was cold and icy, the farthest planet from the sun.

And unlike Uranus, it didn't crack up middle school kids when giving reports on it.

In 2006, Pluto was kicked to the curb by a bunch of eggheads who brushed it off as a mere dwarf planet. As far as Arizona is concerned, Pluto still rocks. Any scientist who doesn't like it can pucker up and kiss the seventh planet from the sun, and that ain't Saturn.

Lowell Observatory was established in 1894, making it one of the oldest in the United States. It may have also been the first time that an observatory was deliberately placed at high elevation in a remote setting (Flag wasn't exactly a metropolis in 1894) for enhanced viewing. It was founded by Percival Lowell, an astronomer from Boston, who would become convinced that there were canals on Mars. Despite years spent searching for life on the red planet, many important discoveries came from Lowell Observatory. Critical maps of the moon were made here during NASA's Apollo Program, and they still carry out planetary mapping, research, and planning. Tours are conducted of the facility. (928) 774-3358, www.lowell.edu.

Clyde Tombaugh also got a much, much closer look at Pluto. Sort of. His discovery would open the door to the vast "third zone" of the solar system known today as the Kuiper Belt. Although Tombaugh died in 1997, a canister of his ashes was aboard the New Horizons spacecraft when it launched in 2006 to make an exploration of the far reaches of the solar system. After 9 years and a journey of 3 billion miles, New Horizons whizzed past Pluto, coming within 7,800 miles, and sent back some amazing photos. It turns out that Pluto, along with its five moons, is much more complex and geologically active than expected. Somewhere in space, Tombaugh must be smiling.

26. Arizona has 15 counties, all of them bigger than Rhode Island.

The original four counties—Mohave, Pima, Yavapai, and Yuma—were formed in 1864 as part of the Arizona Territory. Eight of the counties are named after Native American groups living in Arizona: Apache, Coconino, Maricopa, Mohave, Navajo, Pima, Yavapai, and Yuma. Cochise County is named for the great leader of the Chiricahua Apaches.

Four counties are named for physical features of the Arizona landscape: Gila County for the Gila River, Graham County for Mount Graham, Pinal County for Pinal Peak, and Santa Cruz County for the river of the same name.

Greenlee County is named for Mason Greenlee, an early prospector. La Paz County, the only one formed after Arizona became a state, is named for a historic boomtown on the Colorado River.

Coconino County is the second-largest county by area in the United States. Mohave and Apache are the fifth- and sixth-largest, respectively. Santa Cruz County is Arizona's smallest but at 1,236 square miles, is still larger than 72 *countries*, according to the Arizona Office of Tourism. More than half the state's population resides in Maricopa County.

27. While Europe was mired in the dark ages, cities sprang up across Arizona.

The Ancestral Puebloans were an ancient Native American culture that spanned the Southwest for more than 2,000 years. Their first permanent villages were established around AD 500 as they began to rely less on hunting and more on agriculture. They dwelled in pit houses built mostly underground. Between the years of AD 750 and 900, they began

Keet Seel, built by the Ancestral Puebloans more than seven centuries ago, is considered one of the best-preserved cliff dwellings in the Southwest. Courtesy of Mike Koopsen, Sedona.

constructing large stone-masonry structures, commonly known as pueblos.

Over the next few centuries, the Ancestral Puebloans continued to refine their architectural skills and engineering prowess. Despite the lack of a written language, metal tools, a wheel, or draught animals, they built stone cities atop mesas, in canyons, and set against towering cliff walls. These were highly sophisticated communities that included planned public spaces, many with kivas, large circular rooms used primarily for ceremonial purposes. Hundreds or even thousands of people could occupy the multi-storied apartment-like complexes of these population centers. They were craftsmen skilled in weaving and pottery making, but agriculture continued to be their main economic activity.

Many of the villages were abandoned in the years following the Great Drought (1276–1299). Increasing conflict with Navajo and Apache groups may have also played a part in their migration. The builders of the ancient cities were the ancestors of the modern Pueblo peoples, including the Hopis and Zunis.

28. Arizona has what is thought to be the oldest continuously occupied settlement in the United States.

The ancient pueblo of Oraibi is perched high atop Third Mesa of the Hopi Reservation. The multilevel complex was built by stacking rooms (without ground-level openings) several stories high around a center courtyard. Established sometime before AD 1100, the village has resisted change. Life goes on much as it has for centuries for these patient farmers who live in harmony with their arid landscape. The Hopis are intensely spiritual, a tight-knit community bound together by clan relations. Residents tend to be very private, and photography is prohibited. Please respect their laws, culture, and way of life. To visit one of the villages, schedule a tour with a Hopi guide. www.experiencehopi.com.

29. Arizona has waterfalls higher than Niagara Falls.

Water flows like chocolate in Grand Falls, a massive cascade north of Winslow. In fact, that muddy brown color is why it's also known as "Chocolate Falls." More than 181 feet tall, Grand is higher than Niagara Falls, although not as consistent. It is a torrent during snowmelt and following a hard rain, and just a trickle most of the year. The best times to visit are during March and April. Located on the Navajo Reservation, the road is unpaved. A gravel road is maintained by the Leupp Chapter

House. For current Grand Falls and road conditions, call the Leupp Chapter House at (928) 686-3227.

Mooney Falls, plunging 190 feet in a long column of water, is even taller. Mooney is one of the cascades found amid the otherworldly scenery on the Havasupai Indian Reservation, deep in the Grand Canyon. No one enters the reservation without a permit, and they are very hard to come by. Strenuous hiking is required to reach the various cascades like Havasu Falls, Beaver Falls, and Navajo Falls. But this collection of cascades spilling down rock walls into pools of turquoise water is among the most beautiful waterfalls in the world. www.havasupaireservations.com.

Highest of all in Arizona is Cheyava Falls, another Grand Canyon waterfall. Cheyava plummets more than 800 feet down the Redwall Limestone of the North Rim before dropping into Clear Creek. For much of the year, Cheyava might be little more than a wet streak smearing the canyon wall but during spring snowmelt following a wet winter, it roars to life.

30. The deepest dam in the world spans the Colorado River.

Completed in 1938, Parker Dam is the deepest dam in the world. It has a structural height of 320 feet, but 235 feet are below the riverbed. Deep excavation was needed to reach bedrock. Lake Havasu, the reservoir behind Parker Dam, is about 45 miles long and covers more than 20,000 acres.

31. A woman commanded the Arizona Navy.

Arizona governor Benjamin Moeur really had no choice but to put her in charge. She owned the boats.

In 1934, construction began on Parker Dam. That ignited an uproar leading to a declaration of martial law, a standoff between Arizona and California, and the impromptu formation of the Arizona Navy, which consisted of two wooden ferryboats owned by Nellie T. Bush.

It was the federal government that began building Parker Dam to divert water to southern California. But they had failed to secure permission from Arizona to use its land for the project. Governor Moeur saw it as another attempt by California to usurp Arizona's rightful share of Colorado River water. The governor declared martial law and deployed National Guard troops from Phoenix to make sure that no unauthorized construction took place on Arizona soil.

When soldiers commandeered boats to patrol the river, the Arizona Navy was informally launched with Admiral Nellie T. Bush in command for the days they were afloat. After all, they were her boats.

Despite the fact that one boat got tangled in some cables and had to be freed by the dastardly Californians, the governor's show of force worked. Construction on the dam was halted. At least until the US Supreme Court issued an injunction prohibiting further interference with the dam construction. Water rights would be a contentious issue for decades to come, but for the time being tensions cooled. The Arizona Navy was mothballed.

And don't think for a second that Nellie T. Bush became merely a historical footnote. She was a justice of the peace in Parker, served in the state legislature, and was inducted into the Arizona Women's Hall of Fame.

(*Opposite page*) A group of Arizona residents banded together and spearheaded the preservation movement that saved Route 66. Photo by the author.

32. Arizona saved Route 66.

To put it more accurately, a handful of residents did. It all started in Seligman, Arizona.

Soon after Route 66 opened in 1926, it became known as America's Main Street. For decades, traffic streamed west on the Mother Road, from Chicago to Los Angeles, passing through one small town after another. Businesses thrived as everyone got their kicks on Route 66 in the post–World War II era.

With the expansion of the interstate system, there seemed to be no more need for the old highway. In 1985, US 66 was officially decertified. All signs were taken down, and it was removed from maps. Route 66 ceased to exist. America no longer had a Main Street.

Like many towns bypassed by the new interstate, Seligman struggled to survive. Traffic no longer flowed through downtown; it now roared past on I-40, two miles to the south. Businesses shuttered, residents fled. In 1987, Angel Delgadillo, the town barber, along with his brother Juan, organized a meeting of concerned residents. They formed the Historic Route 66 Association of Arizona, the very first of its kind. They lobbied the state to designate Route 66 as a historic highway, and, lo and behold, they succeeded!

That's how it happened. Arizona provided a blueprint for all other states to follow. That's how the Mother Road exists today, on a state-by-state basis as Historic Route 66. And it's all because a barber in a small town stepped up to save a piece of our heritage.

33. One Arizona town is ruled by burros.

Oatman nestles in the Black Mountains astride Route 66. The former gold mining town is most famous for its four-legged ambassadors. Burros loiter in the middle of the street and collect handouts from travelers. Every day these wild animals come down from the hills to occupy town. Here's the really cool part about that: this wasn't some scheme concocted by the Oatman Chamber of Commerce, Arizona Office of Tourism, or any other agency. The burros initiated the program.

At some point, they said the heck with foraging. Now they visit town each day and stand around blocking traffic while people feed them alfalfa cubes sold in every store. (Please don't feed them anything else.) In late afternoon, just before shops close, the burros mosey back into the hills. They repeat the scenario every day. Where else do critters organize a union and execute a business plan?

34. America's hottest city sizzles on the shore of an Arizona lake.

Winters are deliciously mild in Lake Havasu City. And college students flock to its sandy beaches during spring break. Then summer barges in, all big and boisterous and full of sass. There's nothing subtle about summer here in this sun-spanked land where the Sonoran and Mojave Deserts rub shoulders. Expect plenty of heat. In 1994, temperatures topped out at a scorching 128 degrees in Lake Havasu City. That's a record high for any US city.

Less than 300 miles away, Death Valley National Park holds the record for the hottest place on earth when thermometers soared to 134 degrees back in 1913, but it is not an incorporated town.

35. London Bridge stretches across a channel of the Colorado River in the Arizona desert.

Lake Havasu City might have remained another sleepy retirement community except that traffic increased halfway around the planet, and that made all the difference. In England, the venerable London Bridge, built in 1831, was sinking into the Thames River due to busy city traffic. Rather than demolish the historic bridge, it was put up for sale.

In 1968, Robert P. McCulloch Sr., the founder of Lake Havasu City, bought the world's largest antique for $2.46 million. The bridge used by the likes of Charles Dickens, Queen Victoria, Florence Nightingale, and Jack the Ripper was now on its way to the Arizona desert.

The structure was dismantled, each of the 10,276 granite blocks were numbered, then shipped from London to Arizona, and painstakingly reassembled around a reinforced steel framework to handle all traffic.

London Bridge became the world's largest antique when it was purchased and shipped to Lake Havasu City. Photo by the author.

The deal also included ornate lampposts made from Napoleon Bonaparte's cannons captured at Waterloo. The process took 3 years, and in October 1971, a dedication ceremony welcomed the bridge to its new home.

What may be the most intriguing aspect of the whole saga is just how natural it all seems now. Somehow, London Bridge has been a perfect fit for Arizona's West Coast. Stretching for 930 feet, the bridge connects the mainland to an island in the Colorado River known as Pittsburgh Point. Motorists, pedestrians, and cyclists all utilize London Bridge, which has become Arizona's most popular man-made tourist attraction.

In a land of lighthouses, seagulls, white sandy beaches, and swaying palm trees, London Bridge is just one more happy transplant that found its place in the sun. (928) 855-5655, www.golakehavasu.com.

36. Not only can you fry an egg on the sidewalk in Arizona, but we make a celebration out of it.

Who needs fireworks when you've got street omelets? Every July 4, Oatman holds its beloved Sidewalk Egg Fry. At high noon, participants attempt to make a late breakfast the hard way. Since 1990, the event has been drawing crowds to this former mining town for the festivities. In the early days contestants plopped eggs directly on the sidewalk. That proved to be pretty messy even for a town with mounds of burro poop adorning Main Street. Now the roadside chefs use skillets, pans, or aluminum foil. They're also allowed to utilize mirrors, magnifying glasses, and anything else that might add a few extra degrees of heat, although no fire or electricity is permitted. Costumes are not mandatory, but neither are they uncommon. That's just how Oatman rolls. www.oatmangoldroad.org.

37. Arizona is NOT the hottest state in the country.

Despite the abundant sunshine, the number of deserts, hottest city, and so forth, Arizona does not qualify as the hottest state in the nation. We usually rank somewhere between 5 and 10, depending on what criteria is being used. Why? We go right back to diversity. Lots of cool mountains rise across the landscape. All that elevation moderates the higher temperatures found in the desert. The lowest temperature ever recorded in Arizona was on January 7, 1971, at Hawley Lake, at an elevation of about 8,200 feet, when the thermometer plummeted to a bone-chilling 40 degrees below zero.

Here's another weird fact. Thanks to such diverse climate and geography, Arizona can have both the highest and lowest temperature in the nation on the same day.

If you're wondering which state is actually the hottest, look no further than Florida. That's probably why they snagged the "Sunshine State" motto. Sounds better than the "Sweating Your Butt Off State."

38. There's a lot more altitude than you think.

As mentioned before, we are surprisingly vertical. The mean elevation of Arizona is 4,100 feet above sea level. That covers everything from our lowest spot near Yuma at 70 feet above sea level to the roof of Arizona atop the wind-scoured tundra of Humphreys Peak at 12,633 feet. In between, there's a lot of high country to go around.

With more than half the state sitting at 4,000 feet—mountains and desert in such close proximity—it's never hard to locate the season your heart desires all year-round. Best of all, there are only a handful of days out of the entire year that you can't find 70 degrees somewhere in Arizona. That may be the sweetest fact of all.

39. The largest cottonwood tree in the country grows in Arizona.

The Fremont cottonwood, located near Skull Valley, is a monster. It stands 102 feet tall, with a trunk more than 46 feet around, and a crown spread of 160 feet.

The important riparian species is listed on the National Register of Champion Trees. And don't think for a minute that the big cottonwood is our only representative. While the list is often updated, Arizona generally

Snow frequently falls at Arizona's higher elevations. Courtesy of Mike Koopsen, Sedona.

claims between 45 and 50 national champions—trees that are the largest known examples of their species.

40. Wild horses run free along the Salt River.

It's one of those hold-your-breath moments—to stand on the banks of the Salt River and hear the click of hooves on stone and the rustle of leaves, and then to watch as horses step through the willows, to emerge from the history books and stand in the sun. It feels like you're in Arizona now, watching wild horses graze at the water's edge.

A herd of wild unbranded horses have made a 16-mile stretch of river their home for decades. Advocates say they've been here since before Arizona was a state. They roam the Tonto National Forest near the convergence of the Verde and Salt Rivers, east of Phoenix. Since this is a popular area for kayakers, tubers, anglers, campers, and hikers, the horses have grown accustomed to camera-clicking tourists, so they're fairly easy to observe.

In 2015, when the US Forest Service announced plans to round up and dispose of the herd, it prompted a noisy backlash that made national headlines. Leading the opposition to the plan was the Salt River Wild Horse Management Group, a nonprofit organization that studies and monitors the herd of 100 or so animals. The forest service backed off their plan, and the following year Arizona legislators passed a law providing the Salt River herd with a measure of protection. www.saltriverwildhorsemanagementgroup.org.

41. Navajo Code Talkers helped bring about the end of World War II.

During World War II, 400 Navajo men used their language to create a special code to compose and transmit messages. The code was never broken. These Navajo men participated in every major Marine operation in the Pacific Theater. During the bloody fight for Iwo Jima they fired off more than 800 messages in the heat of battle that were crucial to victory. The code talkers are credited with saving hundreds of thousands of lives and shortening the war.

Sadly, their work was classified for decades. These heroes weren't even allowed to tell their kinfolk what they did during the war. By the time acknowledgment was officially given, they were old men with many already gone. A very moving tribute can be found at the Navajo Code Talker Memorial in Window Rock.

In 2021, National Navajo Code Talkers Day was declared a legal state holiday in Arizona. Each year August 14 will honor the courage of these men and their critical role in the Allied victory of World War II.

The Navajo Code Talker Memorial is located in a tribal park at the base of the sandstone arch, which gives the town of Window Rock its name. Courtesy of Mike Koopsen, Sedona.

42. The first Arizonans were total badasses who brought down mammoths with pointy sticks.

About 13,000 years ago, the earliest-known human inhabitants of the New World were the biggest of the big game hunters. They killed mammoths and bison using nothing but sticks with sharpened stone points. Known as the Clovis people because of that unique projectile point that was first discovered in Clovis, New Mexico, they were nomadic hunters. But their preference for southeastern Arizona around the San Pedro River is unmistakable.

The San Pedro River Valley has the richest concentration of Clovis culture sites in North America. Several Clovis sites are scattered through the valley, the two most prominent being the Murray Springs Clovis Site and the Lehner Mammoth-Kill Site.

At Murray Springs archaeologists identified five buried animal kills that included mammoth, camel, horse, dire wolf, and a dozen bison. Even more significant was the discovery of a Clovis campsite where the kills were processed, hides were worked, and weapons were repaired. The site also contained 16 Clovis projectile points, scrapers, and a wrench-type tool fashioned from a mammoth leg bone. It's the oldest such tool ever found in North America.

The Lehner Mammoth-Kill Site, excavated in 1955–1956, was the first Clovis site to have definable fire hearths and the first where butchering tools were found alongside the remains of animals, including several young mammoths, bison, bear, camel, and tapir. Both Lehner and Murray Springs are part of the San Pedro Riparian National Conservation Area near Sierra Vista, and both are National Historic Landmarks.

43. Arizona is the valentine America gave itself.

Originally part of Mexico, much of the land for Arizona was ceded to the United States after the Mexican–American War in 1848. The southernmost portion was acquired in 1858 through the Gadsden Purchase. Abraham Lincoln formally established the Arizona Territory in 1863. Then it became a long, long wait for statehood. The more genteel eastern half of the country regarded the Western frontier with some suspicion. Too many gunfights and range wars and Gila monsters and general cactus-ness.

Arizona finally became the 48th state on February 14, 1912. That's how it came to be known as the Valentine State. It was the last of the contiguous states admitted to the union.

44. The Arizona state flag totally rocks.

Colorful and eye-catching, the Arizona flag looks dazzling waving in the breeze. A copper star perches on a field of blue. The star identifies Arizona as the largest copper-producing state, and the blue is the same "liberty blue" found in the United States flag. A spray of 13 alternating red and yellow rays fills the upper half, representing the 13 original colonies while mimicking a lavish Arizona sunset.

45. Phoenix is the only state capital with a population over a million.

During Arizona's territorial days, the capital bounced from Prescott to Tucson and back again to Prescott. Phoenix finally became the capital in 1889 through lots of wheeling and dealing—and it stuck, all the way through statehood.

Today, Phoenix is the fifth-largest city in the nation and still growing fast. Its land area exceeds New York City, Los Angeles, and Chicago. The broad swath of desert that comprises the Phoenix metropolitan area is known as the "Valley of the Sun." Sitting at an elevation of 1,086 feet, Phoenix is actually lower than the bottom of the Grand Canyon, which averages out to about 2,200 feet above sea level.

46. Hard to believe, but Phoenix was settled because of the water.

John W. "Jack" Swilling is often called the "Father of Phoenix" because of what he envisioned. Born in South Carolina, Swilling traveled west where he worked as a teamster, prospector, express mail rider, saloon owner, farmer, and public servant. He fought in the Civil War, first for the Confederacy and later for the Union.

In 1867, while riding through the Salt River Valley, Swilling spotted incredible potential. He saw where farms could go, farms with fertile soil and lack of frost. And most importantly he saw a way that water could be distributed. Stretching from the river were the remnants of an ancient canal system that had been built by the Hohokam people.

The Hohokam lived in central and southern Arizona from about AD 1 to 1450. An agricultural society, they created the most complex canal system in ancient North America across the Salt River Basin. More than 135 miles of canals irrigated fields where they cultivated varieties of maize, beans, squash, tobacco, and cotton. The longest of the canals carried water for 16 miles. Although they thrived in the Sonoran Desert for more than 1,000 years, the Hohokam people eventually abandoned the area, leaving behind large villages like Pueblo Grande (now a museum and archaeological park in central Phoenix). Their departure may have been caused by longtime drought.

Jack Swilling moved quickly. He formed the Swilling Irrigation and Canal Company in Wickenburg that year. They went to work digging new canals and reviving old ones. A handful of homesteaders moved in and planted crops. Among that first group of settlers was an Englishman named Phillip Darrell Duppa. He was the one who suggested the fledgling community be named Phoenix since it was a city rising from the ruins of a former civilization.

47. The westernmost battle of the Civil War was fought here.

On April 15, 1862, the westernmost battle of the Civil War was fought on the rocky slopes of a volcanic spire known as Picacho Peak, 40 miles northwest of Tucson. The fierce fighting involved only two dozen men, yet lasted a good part of the afternoon and resulted in a high percentage of casualties—three dead, three wounded, three captured.

It should have never happened at all, but James Barrett, a brash young lieutenant perhaps seeking battlefield glory, disobeyed orders. Barrett was part of the Union's California Column. His squad of cavalry was sent to encircle an encampment of Confederate pickets, along with another unit. Their orders were to capture the sentinels so that the main force of Confederates occupying Tucson would receive no warning.

Instead, Barrett arrived first and immediately charged the Rebel camp. One Union soldier was killed and four others were wounded, with one dying the next day. Barrett was struck by a bullet in the neck and died instantly. Three Confederates were taken prisoner, but the rest escaped after the Union cavalry, exhausted and running low on ammunition, withdrew. There would be no surprise attack on Tucson.

Today Picacho Peak State Park is a popular spot for hiking and camping, and following wet winters, serves up an outlandish display of wildflowers with a sea of golden poppies spilling down the slopes. (520) 466-3183, www.azstateparks.com.

Arizona was also the site of the westernmost skirmish of the Civil War just a couple of weeks before the fight at Picacho. While

On a warm spring day in 1862, the westernmost battle of the Civil War was fought in the shadow of Picacho Peak. Photo by the author.

attempting to slow the advance of the California Column, Confederate soldiers were burning hay piles at Stanwix Station, about 80 miles east of Yuma, when they encountered Union pickets. A few hurried shots were thrown, leaving one Union soldier wounded. That was as far west as any organized Confederate force got during the war.

The man leading the detachment of the Confederate forces was Second Lieutenant John W. "Jack" Swilling, who, in a few short years, would become one of the founders of Phoenix.

48. The bloodiest range war in American history took place in Arizona.

The ironically named Pleasant Valley War made the Hatfield and McCoy feud seem like a minor tiff. Fighting erupted across the high grazing lands below the Mogollon Rim in the 1880s. It began as a dispute between the Grahams and the Tewksburys and took on overtones of the classic cattlemen versus sheepherders antagonism that seemed to color all Western range wars.

The violence eventually ensnared friends and neighbors, with everyone having to choose a side. Hired guns like Tom Horn were imported. Fighting spilled over into the towns, with shootouts in Holbrook and Globe. A gunfight in Holbrook would become one of the most notorious of the Old West. Sheriff Commodore Perry Owens tried to serve a warrant on Andy Blevins, a member of the Graham faction, at his home, which was crowded with relatives. Blevins refused to go and made a move for his gun. Owens was quicker on the shoot and gunned down his man. Others joined the fight, which proved to be a mistake. Owens fired five shots that left three dead and one wounded. The sheriff walked away without a scratch.

Every attack in Pleasant Valley seemed to prompt a bloodier response. The war finally ended, not through any truce, but because nobody was left to kill. In 1892 Ed Tewksbury gunned down Tom Graham on the streets of Tempe. Ed Tewksbury was not convicted, but there were no more Grahams to come after him. The Pleasant Valley War claimed between 20 and 50 lives. Several of the dead men are buried in the cemetery in Young. Historians believe the fighting delayed statehood for Arizona by many years.

49. New Mexico's most famous outlaw actually killed his first man in Arizona.

On a summer evening in 1877, a scuffle broke out in a saloon near the Camp Grant Army Post in southeastern Arizona. The row was between a burly blacksmith named Frank "Windy" Cahill and a skinny teenager working as a teamster whom Cahill had shoved around on prior occasions. After insults were traded, Cahill threw the youngster to the ground. During the scuffle, the teen pulled his pistol, shot the blacksmith in the belly, and fled.

Cahill died the next day. The teamster returned to New Mexico where he became embroiled in the Lincoln County War. More shootings followed, and he soon earned a reputation as a gunman. Yet it was in Arizona that Billy the Kid killed his first man. Just 4 years after putting a bullet in Cahill's belly, the Kid would be gunned down by Sherriff Pat Garrett, dead at the age of 21.

50. The most famous gunfight of the Old West took place in Arizona.

By 1881, Tombstone was the largest city between St. Louis and San Francisco. Despite a cosmopolitan air—the town supported a bowling alley and ice cream parlor—these were violent times. Body counts were so high, it was said that "Tombstone had a man for breakfast every morning."

If that's the case, the town ate hearty on October 26, 1881. That was the fateful day when a long-simmering feud erupted in a narrow vacant lot

A legendary gunfight of the Old West left three men dead in the streets of Tombstone. Photo by the author.

near the O.K. Corral. When the smoke cleared, three men lay dead and three more were wounded.

Tombstone city marshal Virgil Earp appointed his brothers Wyatt and Morgan Earp, along with Doc Holliday, as deputy city marshals on that chilly October day. Wearing black frock coats, under which Holliday concealed a sawed-off shotgun, they strode through the streets to face a group of ranchers and rustlers that included Ike and Billy Clanton, Frank and Tom McLaury, and Billy Claiborne.

The lawmen were there ostensibly to disarm the men who belonged to a loose federation of outlaws known as the Cowboys. Firearms in town were not permitted. Tensions had been high between the two factions for months. The Earps and Holliday came on the Cowboys in a vacant lot, about 100 feet west of the back entrance to the O.K. Corral. Words were exchanged. It's still hotly debated as to who fired first.

Ike Clanton and Billy Claiborne fled as soon as the fight commenced. The violence quickly spilled into Fremont Street. When the smoke cleared, the McLaury brothers and Billy Clanton were dead. Virgil, Morgan, and Holliday suffered wounds. Wyatt was the only participant who emerged unscathed. The most famous shootout of the American West lasted 30 seconds.

Four days after the gunfight, Ike Clanton filed murder charges against the Earps and Holliday. Justice of the Peace Wells Spicer convened a preliminary hearing to determine if there was enough evidence to go to trial. After a month of testimony and a parade of witnesses, Justice Spicer concluded no laws were broken.

But that did not come close to settling the matter. Two months later, Virgil was ambushed and seriously wounded. Soon after that, Morgan was killed with a shot to the back. When no one was charged with either crime, Wyatt took matters into his own hands. With a few friends he set out on his bloody Vendetta Ride, tracking down and killing the men he deemed responsible before leaving the Arizona Territory.

Today, no Tombstone visit is complete without a stop at the O.K. Corral. The property was expanded and now includes the actual site of where the famous gunfight began. Be sure to allow plenty of time to tour the blacksmith shop, the stables, and C. S. Fly's Photo Gallery. The reenactment of the famous shootout takes place daily. The show lasts 30 minutes, an intriguing little skit that ends with a flourish of well-staged carnage. Afterward, the gunfighters are happy to pose for photos. (520) 457-3456, www.ok-corral.com.

51. The world's largest rosebush grows in Tombstone.

This Wild West town isn't all gun smoke and whiskey. There is a softer, more fragrant side that comes out in spring. That's when the world's largest rosebush bursts into bloom. The Lady Banks rose arrived in Tombstone in 1885 as a gift to a homesick bride from her native Scotland. The little rose found the new climate quite agreeable and has thrived. Its gnarled trunk now has a circumference of 12 feet and its canopy covers 9,000 square feet with branches spread across a sprawling horizontal trellis.

The Rose Tree Museum, a former boardinghouse and hotel, shelters the bush and is filled with antiques and artifacts. Each spring the mighty bush is covered in millions of small white flowers. In April, the Tombstone Rose Festival celebrates the bounty of blooms and also includes a parade, live music, fashion show, and high tea. 118 S. Fourth St., (520) 457-3326, www.tombstonerosetree.com.

52. Flowers bloom every day of the year in Arizona. Every. Single. Day.

That may seem like a small insignificant fact, hardly worth mentioning. But for some of us it is reason enough to live in Arizona.

We keep the outdoors handy, and we like it well-decorated with bouquets of flowers scattered about. If you're chasing seasonal blooms, head for the high country in summer when the meadows are adorned with fleabane, blue flax, paintbrush, wild geranium, columbine, and more. Late summer brings on a yellow phase with goldeneye, golden crownbeard, yellow coreopsis, and sunflowers. Long and leggy, sunflowers swipe at clouds and taunt the birds. The plant expends so much energy creating towering stalks it's a wonder they have enough left over to pop

Poppies and lupines bloom on the hills above Bartlett Lake. Photo by the author.

open shiny blossoms. But there they are, waving from roadsides and dancing at the edge of the woods while single-handedly supporting the final days of the butterfly regime.

Autumn brings on a flurry of planting in the desert. Annuals and perennials fill gardens and courtyards and flower beds. Phoenix and Tucson neighborhoods are shaggy with blooms throughout the fall and winter.

Then, while much of the country is still shoveling snow, spring waltzes across the Arizona desert, arriving about Groundhog Day. Blossoms begin appearing often in January and February, heralding our wildflower season—the most spectacular time of year. It can last for weeks, with peak color occurring in March. If enough winter rain spilled, the desert explodes with color. Lupine, owl's clover, brittlebush, globemallow, desert marigold, and their bright-colored ilk all join the festivities.

Of course, the key to unlocking a superbloom year in the desert is whether the Mexican gold poppies arrive in force. Poppies produce satiny, orange-yellow, cuplike flowers atop silver-green foliage. I often refer to poppies as delicate little divas. I love them as flowers but don't think I could stand them as people because they are so high maintenance. First of all they don't even bother showing up unless conditions are perfect. That means rain—and not just run-of-the-mill cloud juice—it has to be specific and personal. It starts with a triggering rain in the fall of an inch or more with consistent rains through the winter. As annuals, poppies have to build a whole plant from seed, and that requires moisture.

After the plants germinate, extreme cold or heat can kill them off. When poppies do finally decide to bloom, they keep banker's hours, if your banker has a drinking problem. The flowers generally open around 10:00 a.m. and close by mid-afternoon. If it's cloudy or too chilly, they don't open at all. I picture them stretched out on a fainting couch telling their assistant to hurry with the tea because they feel a headache coming on.

Yet it doesn't matter how poppies behave. They can get away with anything because they are dazzling and they know it. In those special years, they carpet the desert floor, sweeping around the rocks and saguaros. There will always be people like me willing to drive for hours and hike for miles just to see them gathered together in a group. And to be grateful for the privilege. There's no denying it. I am completely poppy-whipped.

53. Despite their prickly nature, cactus plants produce some of the most dazzling blooms.

Cactus plants may not seem especially complex for much of the year with their snarling spines and waxy menace. But within them beats something wild and beautiful and almost too delicate to believe. They

A pollen-covered honeybee carouses amid brightly hued cactus flowers.
Courtesy of Mike Koopsen, Sedona.

let their freak flags fly in springtime. Eruptions of color burst across the
desert, with April and May being the peak months, extending our wildflower season. The neon pink of the beavertails, the gaudy purple of the
hedgehogs, the bright yellow, orange, and peach of the prickly pears,
and finally the ivory cream of the saguaros. Every plant contributes,
splashing unexpected hues in unexpected places. Blooms generally
last but a single day. It's a brief cycle, but they cram so much passion
into those few hours, I envy them. They are mad for life, drunk with soft
heat and poetry. They kiss the breeze with the softest lips imaginable.

54. Our state flower is fleeting and exotic, and carries on a love affair with bats.

Arizona's official state flower is the saguaro blossom. The big white flowers bloom during May and June, forming a creamy halo atop the cactus

and adding a burst of color at the end of spiny arms. Each blossom is about 3 inches in diameter and emits a pungently sweet fragrance, like melons at a summer picnic.

Yet their time is short. They experience but a single nightfall and one lone sunrise. The flowers typically bloom at dusk and remain open only until midmorning the next day. That nightly schedule is geared toward a very special audience. The lesser long-nosed bats are tiny little things weighing about an ounce, but they are pollinating machines hyper-attuned to saguaros, other columnar cacti, and agaves. The bats will fly more than 1,000 miles along the "nectar trail" through Mexico and into the Southwest, diving over and over into the soft snowbanks of flowers that crown the saguaros.

As the bats probe deep into the blooms with their brush-tipped tongues to gulp nectar, pollen coats their shaggy heads. The pollen then gets spread to other flowers as they make their rounds. The flowers linger for a few hours through the morning. They keep their silken petals flung open wide to greet the day, their last. That allows visitors such as bees, butterflies, and birds a chance to nab any nectar and pollen left behind. And for hikers to grin at the flowers from the trail. All seems right with the world when saguaros are blooming in the Arizona desert.

55. You can eat our state flower.

The saga of the saguaro blossom doesn't end with them just wilting in afternoon sun. Once a saguaro flower has been pollinated, it matures into a fruit that splits open when ripened, revealing red pulp. The fruit provides needed moisture and nutrients for wildlife, which also helps spread saguaro seeds. The Tohono O'odham people have harvested the fruit for centuries by using long sticks to knock it from the cactus. It can be eaten raw or made into a sweet syrup used in jellies and candies.

Now that's a flower!

56. Arizona was the first state with official state neckwear.

We bestowed that honor on the bola tie (sometimes spelled bolo) in 1993. Then in 2007, New Mexico adopted the bola tie as their official state tie. Why? Because they're a bunch of copycats, that's why. Probably still peeved about the whole Billy the Kid thing.

57. The deadliest scorpion in North America hides in our shoes.

When it comes to these ancient arachnids, size really does matter. It's the little guy you have to watch out for. We have one species called the giant hairy desert scorpion, a big lumbering beast that can attain a length of nearly six inches like some kind of mutant shiv-wielding land lobster. Yet its sting is about as painful as one from a honeybee.

The small slender Arizona bark scorpion is the real steely-eyed assassin. Of the more than 1,500 scorpion species, only 25 have venom lethal to humans, and this is one of them, the most dangerous found in North America. While painful, the stings are rarely fatal for humans. Children and the elderly could be in danger, but the antivenin is very effective and widespread. There have been no bark scorpion casualties in Arizona for more than 40 years.

Still, most folks would probably prefer minimizing scorpion encounters. They're nocturnal creatures, feasting on insects, spiders, centipedes, and even other scorpions. Since they can climb and are small, bark scorpions can squeeze through tiny cracks. They occasionally show up indoors, appearing in sinks, bathtubs, closets, shoes, or other nooks and crannies.

If you're the kind of person who enjoys night walks, take a black light with you next time. Scorpions glow in the dark beneath ultraviolet rays,

Spread across the Colorado Plateau in northern Arizona and adjacent states, the Navajo Nation is the largest reservation in the country. Courtesy of Mike Koopsen, Sedona.

turning a blue-green color. It's not the least bit eerie walking out into the dark desert to find yourself surrounded by small glowing radioactive-looking, venom-filled fossils. Then go home, shake out all the shoes in your closet, and sleep tight.

58. The Navajo Nation is the largest Indian reservation in the United States.

Navajoland covers more than 27,000 square miles across Arizona, Utah, and New Mexico. In 2021, it became the most populous tribal nation in the United States with almost 400,000 members. The Navajo capital is Window Rock, located in Arizona. The Navajo Nation is also the only portion of Arizona that observes daylight saving time.

59. Four Corners is the only spot in the nation where you can stand in four states at the same time.

If you ever made a trip out West when you were a kid, chances are this was a stop on your itinerary and you've got the faded photos in a family album to prove it. It's time to upgrade. But this is more than just reliving childhood memories. It's a beautiful drive across the Navajo Nation past colorful canyons and forested mesas to reach this remote spot. Visitors travel from all over to engage in weird Twister-like contortions so they can simultaneously occupy Utah, Colorado, New Mexico, and Arizona. And, of course, to document the moment in a blaze of selfies. Local Navajo and Ute artisans are on hand selling crafts and food. Be sure to stop at the trading post in the nearby town of Teec Nos Pos, a lovely historic business. www.navajonationparks.org.

60. The most photographed slot canyon in the world is carved from slickrock near the shores of Lake Powell.

Nobody knows canyons like Arizona. All across the state, those gouges in the landscape harbor scenery and secrets. The Grand may be the Big Kahuna, but others are also filled with wonders. Located near Page on Navajoland, Antelope Canyon is a sliver of a slot canyon, cut from ancient stone that has been polished to perfection.

The narrow defile features convoluted corkscrew formations shaped by water and wind over millions of years. Curved, rippling walls of glassy stone change colors throughout the day. Beams of light that seem like a living creature pour in from above. This is light that pulses and breathes, striking the sandy floor of the slot canyon in a soft burst. It's like seeing the surprisingly tender skin of the sun.

(Opposite page) Located on the Navajo Nation, Antelope Canyon is accessible by guided tours. Courtesy of Mike Koopsen, Sedona.

The canyon is divided into two separate branches, Upper and Lower Antelope. Navajo-led guided tours enter each section. Upper Antelope is the most popular because visitors walk in on a wide streambed. Pearl-smooth walls close in until it feels like the land itself cradles you. Lower Antelope is longer and highlights its slot-canyon credentials, a snug and winding space. It also requires climbing ladders and steps. Tours file through the narrow confines then climb out via a series of stairs and return by trail. The one-way traffic means less jockeying for photo ops. Peak hours are from 10:00 a.m. to 1:00 p.m., when the sun shafts are most liquid and warm. Solitude may be in short supply, but magic in these slender cathedrals of light and stone is plentiful.

61. Because of a tragedy over Arizona skies, flying became safer for everyone.

June 30, 1956, was one of those beautiful stormy days over the Grand Canyon that people cherish. Rain is always a welcome visitor to this arid region, so hopes arise when great rafts of clouds appear, casting shadows on the cliffs below.

On that morning, United Flight 718 bound for Chicago and TWA Flight 2 on its way to Kansas City both departed from Los Angeles International Airport just minutes apart. Each had experienced pilots at the helm, and their flight plans were different enough that they should have crossed paths without incident. But as a storm system rolled in, the TWA flight received permission to climb above the clouds. At that altitude, the pilot would operate under visual flight rules—the "see and be seen" principle—and would assume the responsibility for spotting and avoiding other planes.

What happened next remains a mystery. At approximately 10:30 a.m., the planes were above the Grand Canyon. It's believed they navigated around the same towering cloud from opposite sides and collided. Later analysis suggested the United flight banked to the right at the last moment, suggesting the pilot suddenly saw the TWA plane emerging from the storm. All 128 people aboard the two planes were killed, making it the deadliest civilian aviation disaster in history to that point.

Yet good did emerge from the tragedy. The crash spurred Congress to step in and repair a strained and ineffective air transportation system. As a result the Federal Aviation Administration was formed and given complete control over American airspace. More air traffic controllers were hired, training improved, and new safety procedures were implemented.

In 2014, the crash site was designated a National Historic Landmark, the first to commemorate an event that occurred in the air. Some wreckage is still scattered in a remote corner of the canyon, and on clear days bits of metal glint in the sunlight, a sad reminder of a stormy day from the past.

Be sure to stop at Desert View on the eastern edge of Grand Canyon National Park. There a stone plaque near the canyon rim pays tribute to the site and the role it played in making the skies safer for one and all.

62. The nation's steepest river thunders down a cliff in Grand Canyon.

At a mere half a mile long, Thunder River is also one of the world's shortest rivers as it gushes forth from a spring deep within the Grand Canyon. It drops 1,200 feet in a series of waterfalls before flowing into Tapeats Creek. So it is also one of the rare instances when a river serves as a tributary of a creek. Backpackers can take the challenging Thunder River Trail from the North Rim to visit this oasis. The trail is only accessible from mid-May to mid-October.

63. The largest dry caverns in the country are found beneath the high grasslands of northern Arizona.

Hidden away amid the high plains and juniper-dotted hills of northern Arizona, Grand Canyon Caverns have been luring Route 66 travelers almost as long as there's been a Route 66. In 1927, a young woodcutter named Walter Peck was on his way to a poker game when he nearly fell into a hole. He returned the next day with his buddies to discover an immense cave. Peck bought the property, believing it to contain mineral wealth. When that proved false, he opened the caverns for tours. Visitors plunked down a quarter for the privilege of being lowered by rope 150 feet into a massive pitch-black hole, thus earning themselves the nickname "Dope on a Rope."

Today, visitors to Grand Canyon Caverns descend in comfort via a 21-story elevator. Guided tours last about 45 minutes and cover three-quarters of a mile, moving through a series of chambers and tunnels. Personable guides lead you through the dramatic depths past flowstone formations and walls glittering with selenite crystals. These are the largest dry caverns in the United States.

Stouthearted guests can also shell out several hundred dollars to spend the night in the Cavern Suite, which has to be one of the largest, deepest, darkest, oldest, quietest motel rooms in the world. Sitting 220 feet below the surface is a comfortable platform room in a chamber 400 feet long by 200 feet wide beneath a 70-foot ceiling. Amenities include a mini-fridge, microwave, television, DVD player, sofa, and two queen beds. I once spent an incredible night in the Cavern Suite, drinking beer and watching old 1950s sci-fi movies about giant spiders and mole people who lived deep beneath the earth's surface. It was great spooky fun. And since dry caverns support no life, I didn't have to worry about bats, rodents, or bugs. It was just me alone in the inky blackness. Wait . . . what was that noise?

The complex also includes a more traditional topside motel and restaurant, RV park, and gift shop. The Caverns Grotto serves lunch inside the cave at cozy tables. The Explorers Tour and Wild Tour allow guests to don hard hats and go clambering and crawling into undeveloped rooms. Grand Canyon Caverns sits 22 miles west of Seligman on Route 66. (928) 422-3223, gccaverns.com.

64. Arizona features the longest stretch of intact Route 66 still in existence.

While much of Route 66 has been replaced by interstate, travelers can still enjoy more than 200 miles of the Mother Road across Arizona. It includes the longest unbroken, intact segment found anywhere between Chicago and LA. That section of historic highway stretches for 158 miles, a long winding river of two-lane pavement beginning near Ash Fork and meandering all the way to the California border. It crosses prairie, mountains, and desert, and passes through small towns and ghost towns beneath big blue skies. This is the crown jewel for Route 66 travelers.

Jump off Interstate 40 at Crookton Road (Exit 139) about 5 miles west of Ash Fork. And that's the last time you'll need to experience freeway travel on this journey. From here on, set your own pace. You're soon greeted by Burma-Shave signs as you ramble through open woodland toward Seligman. Plan to spend a few hours in Seligman, birthplace of Historic Route 66.

You'll cross the wide Aubrey Valley, where one of the original roadside attractions waits. Grand Canyon Caverns offer intriguing tours deep underground. Continue on through Peach Springs and Truxton, with

Stretching across the western half of Arizona, the longest unbroken stretch of Mother Road remains the heart and soul of the Route 66 experience. Photo by the author.

plenty of historic buildings and photo ops. Keepers of the Wild makes a worthwhile stop, at the mouth of Crozier Canyon. It's a nonprofit sanctuary for rescued exotic animals. Tigers, lions, leopards, monkeys and more relax in spacious enclosures spread across rocky hillsides. Always nice to support their good work.

Don't miss Hackberry General Store. A store, museum, and shrine all rolled into one, Hackberry overflows with antiques, memorabilia, old signs, and vintage vehicles. Stop for a cold drink and spend an afternoon browsing the collection.

Be sure to visit with Giganticus Headicus, a 14-foot-tall tiki head who guards the Mother Road on the far eastern fringe of Kingman. As you enter Kingman, you'll find vintage motels, eateries, and a restored train depot. The Powerhouse Visitor Center contains the excellent Arizona Route 66 Museum and gift shop.

From Kingman, the road flashes west across open desert before reaching the rough-hewn Black Mountains. The next 8 miles are a twisting climb filled with hairpin curves and expansive vistas, considered by many, including myself, as the most scenic piece of the Mother Road. It finally levels out on the approach to Oatman. A former gold mining town, Oatman sags in happy repose. Historic buildings fronted by wooden sidewalks are strung along the highway. Gunfights are daily occurrences in the street, and a herd of wild burros will be on hand holding up traffic and seeking handouts of alfalfa cubes.

From Oatman, Route 66 continues through sparse desert another 25 miles to Topock, nestled on the bank of the sparkling Colorado River. Now that's one pure classic road trip.

65. Every astronaut who flew to or walked on the moon trained first in Arizona.

Before NASA could put a man on the moon, they had to drop him off in Arizona first.

During the frenzy of the Space Race, the primary focus was simply overcoming the countless engineering challenges sure to be faced on such an epic journey. Yet at some point NASA realized that if they were going to go to all the trouble of sending a man to the moon, they should really give him something to do when he got there—preferably something with a scientific flavor.

In 1963, the US Geological Survey established their Astrogeology Science Center in Flagstaff. It was created for the geologic study of solid bodies in the solar system. This was a new branch of science. While the astronauts fairly bristled with the Right Stuff, that didn't necessarily translate to a deep understanding of rocks. So NASA began an intensive course in geology.

The astronauts first put in their time in classrooms and then moved on to fieldwork. One of their early field trips was a long arduous hike to the bottom of the Grand Canyon. The 2-day outing gave the astronauts, who were accompanied by geologists, a chance to learn how to identify different strata, detect faulting, see the impact of erosion, and learn geological map reading. They also studied at Meteor Crater and Sunset Crater, among other Arizona locations.

In 1967, the astrogeology team and NASA used explosives to blast hundreds of holes and bowls in the volcanic terrain north of Flagstaff. Known as the Cinder Lake Crater Field, the terrain was designed to simulate Mare Tranquillitatis, future landing site of Apollo 11. Here the astronauts tested spacesuits and equipment, practiced soil-sampling techniques, honed lunar-rover driving skills, and prepared for lunar landings.

Two of the lunar rovers were built in Flagstaff, and one—Grover the Rover—is still on display at the Astrogeology Science Center, where their space exploration work continues.

66. The concept of "life zones" originated in Arizona.

Understanding the staggering diversity of the Arizona landscape doesn't require extensive travel. The distance from the Grand Canyon to the high slopes of the San Francisco Peaks looming above Flagstaff might be just a matter of a few miles, but we know the varied terrain contains multiple life zones.

We know this because biologist Clinton Hart Merriam studied the area in the late 1880s. Born in New York City in 1855, Merriam already had several notable achievements under his belt by the time he arrived on the Colorado Plateau. He had been a naturalist for the Hayden Geological Survey and ornithologist for the US Department of Agriculture. He was also a medical doctor, published author, and one of the founders of the National Geographic Society.

What Merriam found while exploring the rugged landscape between the arid depths of the Grand Canyon, the shady coolness of the ponderosa pine forest, and the bleak alpine tundra crowning Humphreys Peak, Arizona's highest mountain, led to the development of his "life zones" concept. It states that altitude and temperature largely determine what types of plants grow in a particular place.

While widely accepted today, it was a controversial notion when Merriam published his findings in 1890. The theory would go on to change the direction of scientific thought. That's impressive work for a few weeks spent amid the beauty of the Arizona Territory.

67. Tree-ring dating exists because an Arizona astronomer discovered new worlds within the trees.

Andrew Ellicott Douglass was an astronomer who unlocked incredible secrets without ever looking beyond the treetops.

In 1894, amateur astronomer Percival Lowell hired Douglass to choose a site in Arizona for an observatory to study Mars. Douglass found a spot atop a hill in Flagstaff where Lowell Observatory was built. Eventually, the two men parted ways, largely due to Lowell's insistence on seeing evidence of life on Mars that no one else could see. But Douglass was already pursuing a new interest as he researched a possible relationship between rainfall and sunspot cycles. That's when he began studying tree rings in the ponderosa pines surrounding Flagstaff.

Douglass knew that during rainy years the rings were wider, and during times of drought the rings were thinner. He began collecting samples and compiling data. While he was never able to definitively connect the sunspot cycle to tree rings, his work took on a broader scope. By 1929, following years of collecting and cross-referencing specimens, he had compiled a continuous record of tree-ring dating stretching back 1,200 years.

For the first time in history, samples of wood beams could be taken from the ancient Native American ruins of the Southwest to determine when they were built. Douglass had founded the science of dendrochronology, which is the method of dating wood by analyzing the growth ring pattern.

Douglass moved to Tucson and took a teaching post at the University of Arizona. There he founded and directed the Steward Observatory, and later the Laboratory of Tree-Ring Research. Dendrochronology has grown more sophisticated and now reaches much farther back in time. It is used in the study of archaeology, ecology, forestry, paleoclimatology, and chemistry. All because an Arizona astronomer gazed at the stars but never lost sight of the trees.

68. There are more wilderness areas in Arizona than in the entire Midwest.

Almost double, actually. Arizona has 90 wilderness areas, while the Midwest has 51. Only California has more wilderness areas than Arizona. The Wilderness Act of 1964 defines wilderness as "an area where the earth and community of life are untrammeled by man, where man himself is

Hikers journey through Buckskin Gulch in the Paria Canyon–Vermilion Cliffs Wilderness Area. Courtesy of Mike Koopsen, Sedona.

a visitor who does not remain." It established the National Wilderness Preservation System on federal public lands across America.

It has been a special boon to Arizona, where great swaths of backcountry look and feel much like they did a century ago. More than 4.5 million acres here are protected against encroachment and development due to their wilderness designation. At over 800,000 acres, Cabeza Prieta is the largest wilderness segment. Baboquivari Peak is the smallest at a cozy 2,000 acres. A few other wilderness areas include Aravaipa Canyon, Four Peaks, Grand Wash Cliffs, Hummingbird Springs, Mount Wrightson, Paria Canyon–Vermilion Cliffs, Pusch Ridge, Red Rock–Secret Mountain, Strawberry Crater, and Sycamore Canyon.

When the clamor of everyday life gets to be too much, wilderness offers an escape. Hiking, backpacking, kayaking, canoeing, fishing, hunting, bird watching, horseback riding, snowshoeing are all permitted. The forbidden is what allows the silence to unfold and the views to go unobstructed. Motorized vehicles and equipment are prohibited in wilderness areas, as well as mechanized transport (with the exception of wheelchairs). No cars, no ATVs, no dirt bikes, no mountain bikes, no drones. There are no commercial enterprises, no roadbuilding, no power lines, and no permanent structures. It is nature like we remember it.

Wilderness is where you go when you want to hear your own heartbeat again.

69. In Arizona, you can visit an ocean, a rain forest, and a mangrove wetland all in the same day.

Sitting at the base of the Santa Catalina Mountains near the town of Oracle, Biosphere 2 houses seven model ecosystems, earning it the title of the world's largest earth science lab. The University of Arizona runs the facility for research purposes but also offers guided tours to the public. Visitors can wander through a tropical rain forest, savanna grasslands, and even smell an ocean complete with a coral reef.

Looking like a giant mutant greenhouse, Biosphere 2 inadvertently paved the way for all future reality shows. The original plan in 1991 was to seal eight crewmembers inside where they would exist for 2 years solely on what they could grow and produce. Although they did not resort to cannibalism, the experiment fizzled out. Lack of food and oxygen and petty squabbles among the crew eventually sent everyone staggering for the exits. Since being taken over by UA, the scientific research is back on firmer ground. (520) 621-4800, www.biosphere2.org.

70. The Make-A-Wish Foundation began in Phoenix.

It all started with an energetic 7-year-old named Christopher James Greicius, who was being treated for leukemia. In 1980, members of the Phoenix law enforcement community came together to help Chris fulfill his dream of becoming a policeman. He was given a ride in a police helicopter, received a custom-tailored uniform and badge, and was sworn in as an honorary patrolman. Chris died soon afterward, but his dream became the inspiration for the Make-A-Wish Foundation.

A handful of people touched by their experience with Chris formed Make-A-Wish just a few months later. Over the ensuing decades, the nonprofit organization has helped fulfill wishes for hundreds of thousands of critically ill children. The headquarters remain in Phoenix, but chapters have sprung up across the country and all over the world. www.wish.org.

71. An Arizona city has more lighthouses than any other town in the nation.

Now that's a tidbit of information guaranteed to win some bar bets. Not bad for a desert state. You'll find them guarding the water in and around Lake Havasu City. The small structures are scaled-down versions of some of America's most famous lighthouses. Replicas of East Coast lighthouses line the east side of the lake, and ones from the West Coast are re-created on the west side of the lake.

These very stylish navigation towers were designed for boater safety. Built and maintained by the Lake Havasu Lighthouse Club, each of the 28 beacons are about one-third the size of the originals. The first one was erected in 2002, a replica of the lighthouse in West Quoddy, Maine. A map to all lighthouses is available at the Lake Havasu City Visitor Center. 422 English Village, (928) 855-5655, www.golakehavasu.com.

More than two dozen lighthouses line the shore of Lake Havasu and serve as navigational guides for boaters. Photo by the author.

72. The southernmost mile-high city in America perches in Arizona's Mule Mountains.

Blessed with a spectacular setting and old-world architectural flourishes, Bisbee has emerged as a desirable and multifaceted destination garnering national acclaim. Historic and artsy, creaky and classy, Bisbee has evolved into one of Arizona's coolest towns.

At 5,538 feet Bisbee "sits" in the Mule Mountains. Unlike other mountain hamlets that cling to a hillside or nestle in a canyon, Bisbee appears to be spackled into the nooks and crannies of the rugged terrain. Clusters of houses zigzag up cliff faces, defying gravity and common sense. Others flow in and out of gulches and spill over ledges. Narrow streets, often no more than a ribbon of like-minded rubble, curl into the hills and vanish. Some houses can only be reached by stairs. Some stairs can only be reached by other stairs. Think of the least likely spot imaginable to build a town. Got it? Welcome to Bisbee.

Yet it wasn't a skewed sense of humor that prompted such fanciful civic planning. The town sprawled forth out of necessity, straddling one of the richest mineral sites in the world. Mines produced nearly 3 million ounces of gold and over 8 billion pounds of copper, plus silver, lead, and zinc. By the early 1900s, Bisbee's population exceeded 20,000, making it a bona fide Western metropolis.

The inevitable bust followed the boom in the mid-1970s, when the last mine closed. As working folks exited, those of an artistic temperament moved in. Shops and galleries opened; houses and shacks were refurbished, often set ablaze with color. Murals splashed across walls, odd sculptures sprang up in postage-stamp-sized yards, and cars were adorned with paint, sod, and even plastic toys. "Quirky" emerged as the currency of Bisbee's fledgling tourism industry. Today, Bisbee features an array of activities, top-notch galleries, fine dining, and some of the most unique accommodations found in the state. (520) 590-0432, www.discoverbisbee.com.

73. The longest outdoor stair-climb race in the country traverses the hills of an Arizona mining town.

Ready to move beyond the StairMaster at your local gym? Then suit up for the Bisbee 1000 The Great Stair Climb. Every October participants tackle nine staircases with more than 1,000 stairs to surmount, spread over a 4.5-mile course. This isn't jogging up the bland nondescript stairways of a skyscraper or stadium; it's through a worn and weathered mountain town. These winding historic stairs are the concrete bones that hold Bisbee together. Hard-core competitive types come out for the race, but others approach it with a more artistic flair. Plenty of folks show up in costumes. Others just go for the scenic adventure of roaming the hills and seeing a side of Bisbee they otherwise might miss. It's a sweaty home-and-garden tour as well as a race. Bonus: the Annual Bisbee 1000 Craft Beer Festival takes place later that same day, so there's no shortage of refreshment. www.bisbee1000.org.

74. Every time you drink a margarita, you owe a debt of gratitude to Arizona.

On June 6, 1936, the first barrel of tequila produced in the United States rolled off the production line in Nogales, Arizona.

75. We take our drinking seriously.

Blame it on rowdy frontier days. There are entire streets that celebrate the Wild West's love of liquor: Whiskey Row in Prescott, Saloon Row in Williams, and Brewery Gulch in Bisbee.

In Holbrook, Bucket of Blood Street commemorates the former hooch house once called the Cottage Saloon. At least until an 1886 shootout over a card game left two men dead on the floor. Spectators commented afterwards that it looked like a bucket of blood had been spilled and the name stuck. It became the Bucket of Blood Saloon, and those dead card players would not be the only corpses carted off the premises before the saloon closed a few decades later. But the building still stands on the street that bears its name.

Saloons were the foundation of frontier society. The first business that opened in a new town or mining camp was almost always a saloon. They

It only takes a handful of revelers to pack Bisbee's Room 4 Bar, the second-smallest saloon in the country. Courtesy of Rick Mortensen, Cincinnati.

often began in tents or wooden shacks then became more elaborate as the town grew. More than just drinking establishments, saloons served as meeting places, clearinghouses for information, and impromptu town halls. They were also the entertainment districts and online dating sites of their day.

And not much has changed, except along with Arizona's swinging-door saloons we've added craft breweries, distilleries, and wine-tasting rooms in almost every town. Cheers!

76. You can drink in the second-smallest bar in America.

Belly up to the bar isn't just a suggestion in this pocket-sized waterhole; it's a floor plan. The Room 4 Bar in Bisbee holds only four bar stools and a tiny two-chair table, so a basketball team plus coach packs the place.

The 100-square-foot drinking establishment only seems spacious when compared to Key West's Smallest Bar (72 square feet), the nation's teeniest hooch hut.

The Silver King Hotel, a former boardinghouse for miners, has been restored while maintaining the historic integrity of the old building. Five distinctly individual rooms welcome guests. The former Room 4 was converted into the wee saloon. Festivities often spill out into the lobby and onto an adjacent patio. And when bands perform, they set up there so you don't have to worry about a bass player sitting on your lap during a set. 43 Brewery Ave., (520) 432-3723.

77. You can ride a floating tiki bar into the sunset.

Let's face it: Life is too short NOT to spend a day riding across Lake Havasu on a floating tiki bar. The thatch-covered little craft can hold up to six people and has a cruising speed of 4–6 mph as it departs from Lake Havasu City. It's strictly BYOB, so load up on drinks and snacks and head for the open water. Most popular cruises travel through Bridgewater Channel beneath London Bridge into Thompson Bay. Stops can be made at The Turtle Beach Bar if anyone needs a bathroom break or to reload on supplies. Swimming is permitted, and after one of these mini-cruises you'll never want summer to end. (928) 302-2444, www.cruisintikishavasu.com.

78. Even our dead men drink.

On the night of April 8, 1905, John Shaw and William Evans walked into the Wigwam Saloon in Winslow and ordered drinks. Before they quenched their thirst, a dice table piled with silver dollars caught their attention. Guns drawn, they scooped the silver and backed out the door, leaving untouched drinks behind.

Deputy Sheriff Pete Pemberton and Sheriff Chet Houck trailed the outlaws to Canyon Diablo, a once rowdy railroad town. The lawmen arrived at dusk, spotted Shaw and Evans on the street, and everybody slapped leather.

The gunfight was quick. When the smoke cleared, Shaw was dead and Evans was bleeding from multiple wounds. The lawmen emerged unscathed. They loaded Shaw into a pine coffin from the trading post and buried him in a shallow grave. Evans was taken to the hospital in Winslow, where he recovered. (He would later be sentenced to 9 years in Yuma Territorial Prison.) A total of $271 in silver was recovered.

And here's where the story takes a weird turn.

The next night the shooting was a prime topic of discussion among the cowboys at the Wigwam Saloon. What struck the punchers as most unfair is that the boys had paid for drinks and never got to enjoy them. So in keeping with the cowboy code mingled with drunken logic, a gang of fifteen or so men armed with bottles of whiskey boarded the next train for Canyon Diablo. With borrowed shovels from the owner of the trading post in town—he also supplied a Kodak camera—they dug the grave open and briefly resurrected John Shaw.

The sun was just coming up when the cowboys leaned Shaw against a picket fence surrounding a neighboring grave and poured a generous gulp of whiskey through his clenched teeth. They posed for a few photos, two men holding up Shaw between them in a Wild West version of *Weekend at Bernie's*. The photos would be displayed on the walls of the Wigwam Saloon until it was torn down in the 1940s.

While the two very personal pallbearers stand there stone-faced, Shaw sports a knowing grin like he's privy to some secret info. Or maybe he's the only one who sees humor in a situation that's bound to sober anyone up.

They reburied Shaw with the unfinished bottle of whiskey. He might need it on his long journey. Then the cowboys made the train ride back to Winslow, riding east into the velvety light of the early morning sun.

79. A single Arizona curve of the Colorado River will make your eyes pop out.

Since achieving celebrity status on social media, Horseshoe Bend has become one of Arizona's most iconic sights. Viewed from a high cliffside perch 1,000 feet above the water, the Colorado River wraps around a craggy sandstone formation in a swooping embrace. For a moment, the river seems to holds its breath.

Although often identified as part of Grand Canyon, Horseshoe Bend actually lies a few miles east of the national park. This section of river falls within the borders of Glen Canyon National Recreation Area. Up on the rim, a shadeless but short trail (0.6 miles), maintained by the City of Page, is where crowds hike across the sand to a viewpoint unlike any other.

80. The world's largest collection of optical telescopes sits atop a mountain on the Tohono O'odham Nation.

In the 1950s, the search was on for a national observatory. The National Science Foundation considered more than 150 mountain ranges. The site chosen was on Kitt Peak, a high summit in the Quinlan Mountains southwest of Tucson. A lease agreement was reached with the Tohono O'odham people for this use of their land, and Kitt Peak National Observatory was founded in 1958.

Today, Kitt Peak fairly bristles with big space-probing spyglasses

Boaters navigate the Colorado River through Horseshoe Bend, as seen from the overlook 1,000 feet above. Courtesy of Mike Koopsen, Sedona.

boasting three major nighttime telescopes, plus 22 optical telescopes and 2 radio telescopes operated by collaborating institutions. They are, according to the facility website, "the most diverse collection of astronomical observatories on Earth for nighttime optical and infrared astronomy and daytime study of the sun."

81. In 2001, Flagstaff became the world's first "International Dark Sky City."

The designation was awarded by the International Dark-Sky Association (IDA), a nonprofit organization dedicated to protecting and preserving the nighttime environment and the heritage of dark skies. But Flagstaff

Grand Canyon National Park received its Dark Sky designation in 2019.
Courtesy of Mike Koopsen, Sedona.

was just the beginning. Since then several other cities and parks have received the Dark Sky designation. The numbers are always changing as more communities fight to reclaim their night skies, but most of the time, Arizona has more certified Dark Sky Places than anywhere else in the country.

The key has been the systematic elimination of light pollution. Light pollution is defined as excessive or misdirected outdoor lighting. When the light outside runs rampant, it washes out the canopy of stars, planets, and nebulae that were once part of our everyday lives. Almost anyone who lives in an urban environment is submerged in the eerie blaze of brightly lit billboards, stadiums, store signs, and streetlamps. Yet artificial lighting also disrupts the inky blackness above small towns and spills into rural areas. Preserving pristine patches of night sky becomes increasingly important. That's what so many cities, towns, and parks in Arizona are working toward.

Imagine not just a smattering of stars, but a sky so laden it can barely contain them all. A crescendo of stars emerge from the shadows like splintered diamonds as twilight surrenders to the night. The moon plays tug of war with the tides, planets appear, comets blaze across the sky, and wonder of wonders—the long arched streak of the Milky Way stretches overhead. Eighty percent of Americans can't see the Milky Way from where they live. Yet there it is, hovering above Arizona, a river of frosted light. The Milky Way is the galaxy we call home. How nice to be able to connect to it again.

Here are just a few of Arizona's IDA-certified Dark Sky Places:

Sedona	Chiricahua National Monument
Cottonwood	Petrified Forest National Park
Camp Verde	Tonto National Monument
Fountain Hills	Oracle State Park
Grand Canyon National Park	Kartchner Caverns State Park

82. The most famous UFO event since Roswell took place in Arizona.

On March 13, 1997, two events occurred that have become collectively known as the Phoenix Lights. First, a V-shaped pattern of lights flew across Arizona north to south from the Nevada border all the way to Sonora, Mexico, before disappearing. It passed over Phoenix at about 8:30 p.m. Meanwhile, a second set of nine lights seemed to hover above Phoenix for a long period of time. Both occurrences were witnessed by thousands of people and documented with photos and videos.

Governor Fife Symington first tried to dismiss the incident with a joke. Later he would come out and say he not only saw the lights but also believed them to be of otherworldly origin. Actor Kurt Russell, who was flying his plane into Phoenix at the time, claims he saw the strange lights and reported them to the control tower. No official explanation was offered for 4 months. Flares, they finally said. Flares dropped by military aircraft during a training exercise at the Barry M. Goldwater Range near Gila Bend. That's what caused the lights over Phoenix. The V-shaped pattern crossing the state was nothing more than a couple of high-flying airplanes in tight formation, although no one can say whether they were civilian or military.

Those that were looking for logical answers got what they wanted, albeit belatedly. For others, the answers were laughably unsatisfying, and the mystery remains alive. The Phoenix Lights received widespread news coverage, has been the subject of documentaries and books, inspired an alien-themed music festival, and was fictionalized in the movie *Phoenix Forgotten*.

83. Wolves still howl at an Arizona moon.

The Mexican gray wolf is the rarest subspecies of gray wolf in North America. Although they once numbered in the thousands across the Southwest, the wolves teetered on the verge of extinction by the mid-1970s. Authorities captured the last of the remaining wolves to initiate a breeding and recovery program. In 1998, the first 11 wolves were released into the wilderness of Arizona's White Mountains. Although still vulnerable, the initiative has created a small but growing population of lobos in the mountains of eastern Arizona and western New Mexico.

84. Arizona has more species of rattlesnake than any other state.

A total of 13 different species of rattlers call Arizona home, more than anywhere else in the United States. Rattlesnakes are known for their triangle-shaped head and their iconic rattle at the tip of the tail. The rattle is formed by interlocking segments of keratin, the same material that makes up our fingernails. The snakes use the rattle as a defense mechanism to warn potential aggressors to keep their distance.

All rattlesnakes are venomous, but since humans are not their food, they are not out hunting us. In fact, they will try to avoid encounters with people by lying still or trying to escape. (The rattlesnake in the photo stayed perfectly still in the trail as I approached, hoping to go unnoticed. It only rattled its tail and assumed a defensive posture when it felt I was getting too close.) Rattlers won't bite a human unless they feel threatened or provoked. The best way to avoid an unpleasant encounter is to never put your hands or feet in places you can't see. The snakes are an essential part of the ecosystem, a highly specialized predator consuming mostly rodents and small mammals, as well as birds and lizards.

The ridge-nosed rattlesnake is the state reptile. The small snake can be found in the southern mountains of Arizona.

A western diamond-back rattlesnake politely suggests hikers take a wider berth. Photo by the author.

One rattlesnake, pink in color, is found nowhere else in the world except the Grand Canyon. The colorful little creature was brought to the attention of scientists when Eddie McKee, a Grand Canyon National Park naturalist, snagged a specimen. On one of McKee's days off, he was hiking in the canyon when he encountered a rattlesnake that was a strikingly pink color. Realizing it was something he hadn't seen before, he caught the snake by hand and proceeded to hike out of the canyon with it. Please don't try this at home!

McKee reached his car, an old Model T. He couldn't change gears, so he slowly rumbled to the nearest ranger station in first while holding the rattler out the window. Biologists determined it was a previously unclassified species of rattlesnake uniquely adapted to life among the strata of the canyon.

Arizona having more species of rattlers than anywhere else in the United States is also a good nugget of information to have handy when annoying relatives begin hinting at coming for an Arizona visit. Suddenly, the reptiles are EVERYWHERE!

85. The Arizona Cardinals are the oldest continuous franchise in the NFL, dating back to 1898.

86. Only two states offer spring training for Major League Baseball—Arizona and Florida.

The great Chicago Cub Ernie Banks used to say, "It's a beautiful day for a ball game . . . let's play two." That same sense of bubbling joy permeates the Cactus League. It's the time of year filled with promise and possibility. In spring training, every team is in the thick of the pennant race. Budding young stars learn from seasoned veterans, and fans are practically on the field for the action. Before they become the "Boys of Summer," they're just boys in spring, playing a game that is a beautiful blend of skill, drama, and poetry. One that is utterly timeless. Until we're reminded, we forget how baseball forever connects us to our youth.

It started in 1947 when Cleveland Indians owner Bill Veeck, in an effort to avoid racial tension in Florida, moved his team to Tucson. He convinced the New York Giants to relocate to Phoenix, and the Cactus League was born. Veeck signed Larry Doby, the second African American to play major league baseball and the first in the American League. Today, Arizona hosts 15 teams for spring training. And under balmy blue Arizona skies it's always a beautiful day for a ball game. Let's play two.

87. Arizona has the oldest continuously used baseball field in America. Probably.

Wade too deeply into baseball history, and you're bound to stir up controversy. Stat-spewing savants want to argue with you. Ken Burns starts crank calling. Goons sent by Major League Baseball follow you into an alley to pummel you with fungo bats until you promise to never rebroadcast, retransmit, or give an account of the game without express written permission. But perhaps I've said too much.

Warren Ballpark in Bisbee is absolutely historic. That much is certain. The Friends of Warren Ballpark stake their claim to a prestigious piece of baseball history, but also hedge their bets. According to the website, "The ballfield is (arguably) the oldest continuously-operated baseball diamond in the U.S."

They're probably right. The first game was played at Warren Ballpark on June 27, 1909. That's long before the two historic cathedrals of Major League Baseball, Fenway Park in Boston (1912) and Chicago's Wrigley

Field (1914), opened. Yet baseball is a game with multiple eras and leagues and strata to sift through. Other parks around the nation claim to be the oldest. And I don't need Ken Burns heavy-breathing into my phone.

The ballpark was built to provide mine workers and townspeople with a little recreation. It was purposely designed to accommodate baseball, football, and other sports and activities. Warren hosted town, company, outlaw, and semipro teams, with major league teams often playing exhibition games here.

Legends like Honus Wagner, Tris Speaker, Mel Ott, John McGraw, Billy Martin, and Connie Mack have been on the field. Several members of the 1919 Chicago White Sox played at Warren after being banned from professional baseball for fixing the World Series. Bisbee teams have been farm clubs for the Los Angeles Angels, Chicago Cubs, and New York Yankees.

Today, the Copper Classic, a vintage baseball game, is played to raise funds to help with the restoration of this historic gem. The park also hosts music festivals and other events. High school baseball and football teams battle it out through the seasons at Warren, which has also been called the oldest minor league ballpark in the country, and the oldest operational multiuse sports park in the United States. www.friendsofwarrenballpark.com.

88. Arizona women gained the right to vote in 1912, 8 years before national suffrage.

While Arizona was still a brand-spanking-new state, a handful of women spent the hot Arizona spring and summer of 1912 going door to door—at a time when doors were often far apart—collecting signatures. By July, they had more than enough to get women's suffrage on the fall ballot. When November rolled around, the voters (all men) overwhelmingly approved. Arizona became the 10th state to allow women the right to vote. All of the states were in the West.

This was a land newly settled, with women sharing the work and building communities. It wasn't much of a stretch for them to be granted the right to vote. In 1920, when it finally came time to ratify the 19th Amendment, which granted women across the nation the right to vote, there were already four women serving in the Arizona Legislature and leading the way.

89. Some of the oldest trees on earth can be found in Arizona.

These are trees that once shaded dinosaurs. These ancient stone trees lie tumbled and broken amid the colorful badlands and short-grass prairie of Petrified Forest National Park.

During the Triassic period, this was a humid forested basin. Crocodile-like reptiles, giant amphibians, and some of the earliest dinosaurs roamed among towering trees and leafy ferns. As the trees died they were washed into the swamps and buried beneath volcanic ash, where the woody tissue was replaced by dissolved silica, which eventually formed petrified wood. Nearly a dozen species of fossilized trees have been identified in the park. All are extinct. A scientific bonanza of plant and animal fossils has also been unearthed here.

In 1906 President Theodore Roosevelt used the Antiquities Act to create the Petrified Forest National Monument, 2 years before granting the same designation to the Grand Canyon. Serving as a world-class scientific laboratory, Petrified Forest became a national park in 1962.

The fallen trees of Petrified Forest National Park date back more than 200 million years. Courtesy of Mike Koopsen, Sedona.

Brilliantly colored petrified wood is Arizona's official state fossil. Don't disturb or collect any fragments you find in the park. Petrified wood gathered on private property is for sale at numerous rock shops.

Petrified Forest lies east of Holbrook. Take the 28-mile scenic drive that cuts north to south, connecting park highlights from roadside vistas to historic sites to hiking trails, and a lovely Route 66 memorial. Don't miss Blue Mesa, a loop road skirting colorful badlands. Some of the best displays of petrified logs can be seen along the short Crystal Forest Trail. (928) 524-6228, www.nps.gov/pefo.

90. Naturally, we have the world's largest petrified tree.

It stands—yes, stands—outside a gift shop near Holbrook. The tree, weighing some 80 tons, was discovered on the property of the Geronimo Trading Post. It was dug up and partially reburied out front near the parking lot as an irresistible tourist attraction. It stands upright more than 10 feet tall, big and broad, a great photo op, unless you're somehow able to the resist the urge to stand next to the world's largest anything. If so, what kind of traveler does that make you? Geronimo Trading Post is at Exit 280 off I-40, about 5 miles west of Holbrook.

91. Camp Verde is home to the world's largest kokopelli.

Kokopelli, the humpbacked flute player, is a Native American symbol of fertility, a rainmaker, storyteller, and bringer of joy. The prehistoric deity has been depicted in ancient rock art for more than a thousand years. Such a cheerful, playful spirit continues to be celebrated in modern times. Kokopelli has become an enduring symbol of the Southwest.

The Camp Verde kokopelli can be found just east of Interstate 17 in front of a row of shops. He stands 32 feet tall and is painted bright yellow. Made of welded steel and weighing 5.5 tons, the merry minstrel is built to last and will serenade travelers for years to come.

The world's largest kokopelli serenades Camp Verde visitors. Courtesy of Mike Koopsen, Sedona.

92. The world's largest desert tortoise resides in Bullhead City.

He weighs 2 tons and is named Poki. The big fellow stands guard outside the Bullhead City Chamber of Commerce. A local resident commissioned the giant sculpture for his private property but later donated it to the town. Poki sports a sly smile, like maybe someone once told him a good tortoise joke and he's just now, slowly, slowly—so slowly—beginning to grasp the punch line.

93. The world's tallest kachina doll stands just a few miles away from America's largest sundial.

It's only proper the sunniest state should have the nation's largest sundial. You'll find it in Carefree. Designed in 1959 by solar engineer John Yellot and architect Joe Wong, it stretches for 62 feet and points to the North Star. When built it was the largest sundial in the entire world, but it has since been, if you'll pardon the expression, eclipsed.

The world's largest kachina doll towers over the sleepy subdivision of Tonto Hills, a few miles east of Carefree. The 39-foot-tall version of a traditional Native American carving can be found just off Cave Creek Road.

94. We know how to celebrate New Year's Day with some panache.

The New Year is rung in by dropping a giant pine cone in downtown Flagstaff, a cowboy boot on Whiskey Row in Prescott, a taco in Tucson, and a head of lettuce in Yuma. How do you like them apples, New York City?

95. The country's largest and second-largest man-made lakes can be found here.

They both stretch along the state's northern border. The largest—Lake

Houseboats seek out secluded coves amid the endless miles of Lake Powell's shoreline. Courtesy of Mike Koopsen, Sedona.

Mead—was formed after the completion of Hoover Dam. Lake Powell came about with the building of Glen Canyon Dam. At full pool, which sadly we haven't seen for a long while, Lake Powell has 1,960 miles of shoreline.

96. The only freeway in the United States that uses metric signage is here.

Running north to south between Tucson and Nogales on the Mexican border, Interstate 19 is short, scenic, and unique. Distances along I-19 are marked in kilometers instead of miles. I-19 provides access to the communities of Green Valley, Sahuarita, Tubac, and Rio Rico, as well as Mission San Xavier del Bac and Tumacácori National Historic Park.

It's one of the country's shortest freeways with a total length of just over 63 miles. Oops, make that 102 kilometers.

Speed limits are still kept at miles per hour, thank heavens. Otherwise, you'd have people careening down the highway doing 130, not noticing that the sign was marked KPH instead of MPH.

97. Islands float across southern Arizona.

Stretching from Mexico into Arizona, a series of mountain ranges forms an exotic high boulevard between the subtropical Sierra Madre to the south and the temperate Rocky Mountains to the north. These are the Sky Islands, harboring the type of biological diversity that exists nowhere else in the country. Forested mountaintop islands are surrounded by seas of desert and grasslands creating tightly stacked ecosystems, distinct and isolated. Here you'll find more than half the bird species in North America and the highest concentration of mammals in the United States. Entomologists have found evidence suggesting there may be more species of ants and bees in the Sky Island region than anywhere else on earth. This is our rain forest, a hotbed of life.

Some of the Sky Island mountains rise more than 7,000 feet above the desert floor, with different life zones occurring at varying elevations, each with its own specific array of plants and animals. Many endemic species are trapped on individual mountain ranges, evolving in isolation. Other species use this unique crossroads to stretch the limit of their range. The Sky Islands are the northernmost outpost for the likes of the jaguar, ocelot, brown vine snake, Sonoran tiger salamander, and elegant trogon.

98. Ecologically, you can drive from Mexico to Canada in about an hour.

You can do it twice if you want. Both the Sky Island Parkway to the top

The columns and spires of Chiricahua National Monument crown one of Arizona's prominent Sky Islands, harboring an incredible diversity of plant and animal life. Photo by the author.

of Mount Lemmon and the Swift Trail up the slopes of Mount Graham travel through five life zones, from Sonoran Desert lowlands all the way up to mixed conifer forest, the ecological equivalent of driving from Mexico to Canada.

The Sky Island Parkway in Tucson proves another weird but wonderful Arizona fact. You can ski and swim in the same day. Make the winding 27-mile drive on a winter morning rising above the lanky saguaros through grasslands and oak trees into the pine forests mingled with aspens. Take a few runs on the slopes at Ski Valley, polish off a hot cocoa, and you can drive back to town and be swimming in a backyard pool that afternoon, where the temperatures could be 30 degrees warmer.

The Swift Trail is a more rustic experience near the small town of Safford. It's a narrow country road with sharp twists and turns, and is unpaved at the top. This is a summer drive because the upper portion of the road is closed from November 15 through April 15. It's 35 miles to the top of Mount Graham, where you'll find alpine meadows and sparkling Riggs Lake, ringed by forest, a very different world than the one you left below.

99. Mount Lemmon is the southernmost ski resort in the United States.

100. An isolated range of Arizona mountains are the most diverse mountains in North America.

The Pinaleño Mountains are a wall. Steep and sudden, they tower above the small towns of Pima, Thatcher, and Safford in southeastern Arizona. They have over 7,000 feet of vertical relief, more than any other range in the state. The Pinaleños are the tallest of Arizona's southern Sky Islands, with peaks higher than 10,000 feet in elevation. That rapid rise from low to high means they are stacked with five distinct ecological communities, including 18 species and subspecies of endemic plants and animals found nowhere else on earth. According to the Nature Conservancy, the Pinaleños contain the highest diversity of habitats of any mountain range in North America.

101. The southernmost spruce-fir forest in the United States crowns Arizona mountains.

As previously stated, the Pinaleños are a towering range, anchored by Mount Graham at 10,720 feet, which happens to be the southernmost

A monsoon storm darkens skies above the red rocks of Sedona. Courtesy of Mike Koopsen, Sedona.

peak in the continental United States above 10,000 feet. Desert wraps around the base of the mountains, but that changes drastically in just 4 linear miles. The highest elevations support the most southerly Engelmann spruce–corkbark fir old-growth forest in the United States. It's the only true spruce–fir forest in the Sky Islands. Amid the extensive forests and alpine meadows, you'll find a heavy population of black bears and the Mount Graham red squirrel, a subspecies that only exists here.

102. We have five seasons.

Let's face it; four seasons just aren't enough for Arizona. We need a fifth one, a special one, one full of drama, hope, and the promise of magic. We need a season with the power to transform our whole world.

We need monsoon season.

Rolling in on the heels of scorching summer days, monsoon season is far more ethereal than our traditional equinox-defined seasons. Once upon a time it was declared official by consecutive days of dew points above 55, but that proved to be too nerdy. So monsoon season was assigned its own specific dates. It now begins each year on June 15 and ends on September 30.

Of course we all know that calendars mean nothing to monsoon. It operates on its own schedule, appearing haphazardly, off and on in sudden bursts and breaks. Often it seems to occur everywhere except where we happen to be. But in those wonderful years when it arrives in all its splendor, when it brings a deluge of rain to each corner of the state, everything seems right with the world.

Yet rain is only a part of this complex weather festival. All the elements of monsoon storms are thrilling. They drop the temperature as chilled air swoops in and snatches away our summer sizzle. There's no better feeling than running around the house on an August afternoon and flinging open windows so that a cooling breeze can come in with a whoosh. For a few delicious minutes, the air feels sweet and juicy as tree-ripe peaches.

Then we gaze toward the heavens. Monsoon storms unleash a cosmic opera of shadow and light. Half the sky goes black. It's like Midnight showing up uninvited to brunch. An armada of seething dark clouds jostles for position while the saguaros below are bathed in white sunshine. As the storm closes in, the light turns reckless and wild, and there's that moment of anticipation as we stand on porches wondering if the system will break apart and vanish, or if it will hold together long enough to deliver our salvation.

Then the sky quivers and those first drops fall—sparse and scattered and as fat as cherries. That opening salvo is just a prelude, because soon a seam splits open and rain pours down in a frothy cascade. It comes fast and ferocious, a silver veil connecting land and sky in a long-awaited reunion. Harmony is restored.

Rain creates its own special fragrance in Arizona—a haunting perfume that smells like home to many residents. Courtesy of Mike Koopsen, Sedona.

Life is granted an extension because of rain. Plants wiggle their roots in glee. The cacti swell up. Seedlings and blossoms that have been on indefinite hold suddenly flourish. The desert turns almost instantly green—green enough to make leprechauns book their Arizona vacation.

Then there is that unforgettable smell . . .

103. Our rain smells heavenly.

It's easy to overlook creosote in the desert. The plants often grow where nothing else will, and are spindly but tough. They produce a wild spray of thin branches, each covered with small waxy leaves. When that waxy oil gets wet, it releases a very special and pungent aroma—one that you never forget, with notes of hope, joy, and contentment woven in.

If there is a more seductive perfume than rained-on desert, I don't know what it could be. It's a fragrance that means home to Arizonans.

Those big fat raindrops kiss the ocotillo, dance among saguaro spines, and water our vast herd of lizards. And while that's happening the land unleashes a musky, earthy fragrance, all heart-meat and hyacinth. Scientists have named the aroma petrichor. But it is so much more than the smell of wet creosote. It is angel breath. It is the scent of almost forgotten love. It is the juice of a billion stars, a flavor intoxicating, comforting, and evocative. When rain falls in the desert, you can feel the earth smile.

For a while, we get to believe in miracles again. Anything seems possible. It has rained in the desert.

104. Arizona is Hollywood's open-air back lot.

More than 5,000 movies and television shows have been filmed in Arizona. Here are just a few.

Return of the Jedi

Indiana Jones and the Temple of Doom

Forrest Gump

Psycho

Easy Rider

The War of the Worlds

Stagecoach

Tombstone

Planet of the Apes (1968)

Planet of the Apes (2001)

Raising Arizona

The Outlaw Josey Wales

Bill & Ted's Excellent Adventure

Eight Legged Freaks

The Shawshank Redemption

A Star Is Born (1976)

Into the Wild

Rio Bravo

The Greatest Story Ever Told

Starman

Revenge of the Nerds

Jerry Maguire

Bus Stop

How the West Was Won

Wayne's World

Piranha 3D

The Karate Kid

Midnight Run

Tin Cup

Oklahoma!

105. Truth is, Arizona was supposed to be Hollywood.

In 1913, Cecil B. DeMille was looking for a place to shoot a Western called *The Squaw Man*. He was living in New York City at the time, so he decided to travel to the most Western of states. But perhaps he made the same assumption that so many do about Arizona—it's all desert. He took a train to Flagstaff.

In December.

DeMille stepped off the train on a cold day in the tall pine forest at 7,000 feet elevation. Not what he had envisioned for his first film. He reboarded the train and continued onto Los Angeles. He rented a barn in Hollywood and began filming his movie. *The Squaw Man* was finished by January 20, 1914, and was wildly successful when released. He moved the barn to United Studios, which soon became the home of Paramount Pictures. Hollywood had a new industry.

Now suppose DeMille had taken the train into Phoenix, or Tucson, on that December day. Gazing across a forest of bristling saguaros framed by rugged mountains beneath a radiant blue sky, do you think he would have decided that scenery wasn't Western enough for a Western?

106. We are the very definition of wide-open spaces.

One of the reasons Hollywood directors like us is because we keep our horizons spread wide, allowing for all sorts of action in between them. Approximately 82 percent of Arizona's land comprises national forests, national parks, wilderness and recreation areas, state trust land, wildlife refuges, and Indian reservations.

A hiker enjoys some of Arizona's distinctive wide-open spaces. Courtesy of Mike Koopsen, Sedona.

107. Phoenix is no Gotham City, but it does have a bat cave.

Just as the sun slips beyond the horizon and the shadows deepen, the bats emerge. A fluttering, flapping, squeaking swarm launches from the tunnel, maybe 10,000 to 20,000 of them. They take to the desert sky, gobbling insects by the ton. Not a sight you expect to see in an urban environment, but bats play by their own rules. After all, they're mammals that decided to master the power of flight.

Since the 1990s, thousands of Mexican free-tailed bats migrate from south of the border to spend the summer in a flood control tunnel near 40th Street and Camelback Road. No one knows why they picked this particular tunnel, but they're obviously happy enough with the accommodations to return each year starting in March. The full colony is in place by June. Females give birth in the tunnel, one pup per season. They'll roost in the tunnel by day then fly out each evening to forage for food. On any given night, free-tailed bats will travel up to 20 miles to feed. Each bat can consume thousands of moths, beetles, mosquitoes, and their pesky ilk. Best times for viewing are June through August, but they can still be seen as late as October before the last stragglers pack up and head south for the winter.

Spectators gather most nights through the summer for the twilight ballet. Remain still and quiet and enjoy the show. Surprisingly, the bats will not suck your blood or tangle in your coiffure. Once again Hollywood portrayals are not pinpoint-accurate.

The tunnel is north of 40th Street and Camelback Road. The path to the tunnel is located on the north side of the Arizona Canal. Follow the canal west for about 200 yards, past office buildings and a parking garage. A paved path to the right will take you to the top of the tunnel. Bats will make their exit just after sunset.

108. Arizona has more species of bat than any other state—except Texas.

There are 28 species of bats that live in the state at least temporarily. Canyon bats are the smallest of the flying mammals in the United States, weighing about as much as a nickel. They're usually the first bats seen in the evening. Their flight is erratic and wobbly, so they often look like butterflies in fur coats.

109. The nation's first federally protected archaeological site stands tall in the Arizona desert.

Casa Grande Ruins is the centerpiece of an ancient Hohokam community. The Hohokam people farmed much of central Arizona, including

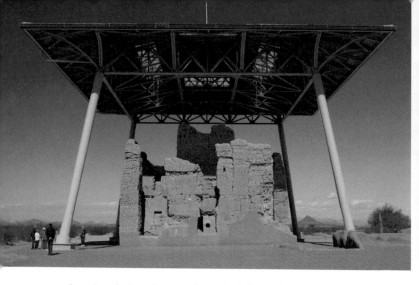

Casa Grande Ruins became the nation's first archaeological reserve in 1892.
Courtesy of Mike Koopsen, Sedona.

the flat plain between the Gila and Santa Cruz Rivers near Coolidge.
They also found time to build a veritable skyscraper out of mud, an
imposing four-story structure that looms over the remnants of the
village. On June 20, 1892, President Benjamin Harrison proclaimed the
site as Casa Grande Reservation. It was the first prehistoric and cultural
reserve in the United States. President Woodrow Wilson re-designated it
a national monument in 1918.

Standing 35 feet tall, Casa Grande, or "Big House," was built of unre-
inforced clay (caliche) in the mid-1300s, a massive project requiring tons
of building material and a large labor force. The purpose of the towering
structure has never been determined. A reinforced steel ramada was
built in 1932 to shelter the ruins, replacing an older wooden one. Yet
somehow the Big House survived seven centuries of scorching sun and

extreme weather all on its own. Also on the grounds of Casa Grande Ruins National Monument are an excellent museum, several smaller structures, and a ceremonial ball court. Guided tours are offered as staffing permits. (520) 723-3172, www.nps.gov/cagr.

110. Criminals in Wickenburg were sentenced to sit outside in the shade.

It wasn't exactly Alcatraz or Yuma Prison, but at least no one ever escaped. From 1868 to 1890, legend says Wickenburg scofflaws were chained to a mesquite tree that served as the town hoosegow. Of course, it was only a holding facility, a place to keep prisoners secure until a lawman from Phoenix could ride up and fetch them. Although that could take anywhere from two to five days.

The 200-year-old mesquite is located at the corner of Tegner Street (US 93) and Wickenburg Way (US 60). There is some informational signage and even the life-sized sculpture of a forlorn prisoner shackled to the trunk. It still seems like a decent spot to do your time. Getting a splinter is not as bad as a shiv.

111. We captured public enemy number one.

During the latter part of the 19th century, Arizona had plenty of experience dealing with outlaws on the streets. When it happened a few decades later it made national headlines. In January 1934 the Tucson Police Department, with an assist from the Tucson Fire Department, did something the FBI could never manage. They captured John Dillinger.

When a fire broke out in the Hotel Congress, everyone was evacuated. Two guests pleaded with firemen to rescue some very heavy luggage. They tipped the firefighters $12 for their trouble. Later that day, back at the station, while thumbing through an issue of *True Detective* magazine, the firemen recognized the big spenders as members of the Dillinger gang. Turns out, the gangsters were soaking up the winter sun in Tucson. A short stakeout resulted in the capture of Dillinger, whose car was loaded with weapons and cash. Not a shot was fired. Also apprehended were Harry Pierpont, Charles Makley, and Russell "Art" Clark.

The historic Hotel Congress, now at the heart of Tucson's vibrant downtown music and culinary scene, commemorates the event with a 2-day party each January. Dillinger Days features a speakeasy, reenactments, food and music, tours, and lectures. 311 E. Congress St., (520) 622-8848, hotelcongress.com.

112. The most feared penitentiary of the Old West is also one of America's most haunted locations.

Carved from a granite cliff overlooking the Colorado River, Yuma Territorial Prison was America's most notorious 19th-century calaboose, housing some high-profile inmates like Buckskin Frank Leslie and Pearl Hart. The prison opened in 1876, and by the time it closed 33 years later had earned a fearsome reputation. It's now preserved as an Arizona state park.

In 2018, Yuma Territorial Prison was named the country's most haunted destination by a USA Today's Readers' Choice Award. No one was executed at the Yuma pen, but 111 prisoners died while incarcerated and 104 still lie in the sunbaked prison graveyard. Visitors can explore the stark cellblocks, walk among the lonely graves, climb into the guard tower, and feel the walls close in around them in the infamous "snake den" punishment cell. The museum is filled with artifacts and exhibits. (928) 783-4771, www.yumaprison.org.

Inmates who mis-
behaved at Yuma
Territorial Prison
were confined
to the Dark Cell,
also known as
the "snake den,"
a small cave with
an iron cage in
the middle. Photo
by the author.

113. **Every Yuma high school student has a criminal record.**

Yuma High School was established in 1909. It started with 4 teachers in 3 rooms and 12 graduating seniors. The next year the high school was forced to move, either because of a fire or simply a lack of space. For their new home they chose the abandoned Yuma Territorial Prison.

Classes were held in the old cellblock, and assemblies took place in the former prison hospital. When the city decided they wanted to repurpose the prison for a jail, a new high school was built in 1913. That same year, the little ragtag Yuma football team traveled to Phoenix where they beat the Coyotes in a startling upset. Phoenix fans began taunting the opposing players for being a "bunch of criminals." It may have rankled at first, but soon Yuma students wore the name with pride. In 1917, the school board made it official, adopting the name and a roguish-looking mascot wearing prison stripes. Yuma High School has been the home of the Criminals ever since.

114. During World War II, the German version of *The Great Escape* took place in Phoenix.

During World War II, Camp Papago Park was constructed to house American soldiers undergoing desert combat training. But an influx of prisoners of war led to a repurposing of the facility in 1943. Italian prisoners were initially held before being transferred to camps in California. The first German POWs arrived in January 1944.

On December 23, 1944, under the cover of darkness, 25 German prisoners of war tunneled out of Camp Papago Park and scattered across the desert. It was the largest escape by Axis prisoners from a United States compound during the war.

The Great Papago Escape, as it was called, caught the Americans by surprise, coming as it did via tunnel. Officials believed it was impossible to dig through the decomposed granite of the grounds. Yet the industrious Germans carved a tunnel that started behind a bathhouse and stretched for 178 feet. It went under two fences and a road before emerging on the banks of the Crosscut Canal. Excavated dirt was hidden in attics, flushed down toilets, spread in gardens, and eventually used to build a faustball court, a game similar to volleyball.

All of the escapees were Navy personnel. Three of them built a small boat with plans to raft down the Gila River to Mexico. They were dismayed to discover that Arizona rivers were often more implied than real. Despite the blue line shown on the gas station map one prisoner had managed to swipe, the Gila consisted of only a few languid puddles. All prisoners either surrendered or were recaptured within a few weeks.

115. Arizona has the most famous corner on all of Route 66.

Sitting on the high plains of northern Arizona, Winslow started out as a railroad hub. That tailed off after World War II, but then things boomed

Travelers come from all over the world to stand on a corner in Winslow, Arizona, the most famous corner on all of Route 66. Photo by the author.

during Route 66's heyday. Once Interstate 40 bypassed the town, Winslow began to wither. But then it redefined itself yet again, all thanks to a line in a song that was written by Jackson Browne and Glenn Frey and released in 1972. "Take It Easy" became the first big hit for Frey's band, the Eagles, peaking at No. 12 on the Billboard chart that summer. The iconic second verse begins, "Well, I'm standing on a corner / In Winslow, Arizona . . ."

In 1999, the town of Winslow re-created the musical tableau from the song. They commissioned an artist to build a life-sized bronze sculpture of a long-haired troubadour and his guitar, which they placed on a downtown corner. Behind him, a mural was painted on the side of the building filling in the missing pieces to the story. There's the name,

Winslow, Arizona, in big letters. There's the girl in a flatbed Ford flashing the flirty eye. There's even an eagle perched on a ledge, overlooking the scene. The building burned in 2004, but the wall with the mural survived in what is known officially as Standin' on a Corner Park.

People travel from all over the world—anywhere up to 100,000 visitors every year—to insert themselves in that musical moment. They come here to stand. On a corner. In Winslow, Arizona. Because of a song echoing out of their past, a moment from their youth that somehow resonated with them. That's the power of music.

When Glenn Frey passed away in January 2016, the city of Winslow wanted to honor him. They commissioned a new bronze sculpture that was added to the corner. RIP, old friend. Or better yet, take it easy.

116. The first federally funded interstate highway in the Southwest was built with a brigade of camels.

In 1857, Lieutenant Edward Fitzgerald Beale was chosen by President James Buchanan to survey and build a wagon road across lands acquired after the Mexican–American War. Twenty-two camels were provided to carry supplies for Beale and his men across the largely trackless wilderness.

Although skeptical at first, Beale developed an appreciation for the camels and their abilities. He even wrote, "I look forward to the day when every mail route across the continent will be conducted and worked by this economical brute."

That didn't pan out. The mule skinners with the Beale expedition did not approve. They considered the camels bad-tempered and foul smelling. Which raises the question . . . just how pungent do you have to be to offend the delicate olfactory sensibilities of mule skinners?

While the camel experiment fizzled, Beale's wagon road was a resounding success. Thousands of immigrants and livestock numbering in the millions traveled the path over the next 30 years. When completed, it provided a serviceable route for 1,240 miles, from Fort Smith, Arkansas, to the Colorado River. The price tag was a meager $210,000.

The transportation arteries that came later—the railroad, Route 66, and Interstate 40—all followed the course of Beale's modest wagon road. Today, the section that passes through the Kaibab National Forest is maintained as a 23-mile stretch of recreational hiking trail. The route makes use of forest roads and trails that have been marked with rock cairns, tree blazes, and wooden posts. There are plans to build trailheads and add more signage. Laws Spring is the major access point and a designated parking area along the Beale Wagon Road. (928) 856-5600, www.fs.usda.gov/kaibab.

117. Arizona produces more copper than all the other states combined.

The Morenci Mine is the largest copper producer in all of North America. It transitioned from an underground mine to one of the largest open-pit mines in the world. Owned by Freeport-McMoRan, the Morenci mining fleet of haul trucks and shovels can move an average of 815,000 metric tons of material per day. This seems like a good time for a reminder that the 5 Cs of the Arizona economy are Cotton, Citrus, Cattle, Climate, and Copper.

Sexy metals started it. Early Spanish, Mexican, and American prospectors dug for gold and silver, and plenty of that was found. Tombstone, for example, was a legendary silver strike. But no ore was as widespread or enduring as copper. Once the railroads arrived in the late 19th century, mining and shipping copper became profitable. Other booming copper mines (with some still active) include Bisbee, Jerome, Globe-Miami, Ray, Safford, and Bagdad. Arizona's first open-pit copper mine began operation in Ajo in 1917.

118. The first steel dam in the world was built in Arizona.

Steam locomotives were thirsty beasts. Crossing an arid land required reservoirs to be created near the tracks to provide water for the trains. In 1898, the Atchison, Topeka, and Santa Fe Railway built a steel dam in remote Johnson Canyon east of Ash Fork. Francis Bainbridge, a civil engineer working for the railroad, created the unique design. The Ashfork-Bainbridge Dam was constructed with 24 curved plates, giving it a scalloped appearance.

While the steel dam proved to be much cheaper and faster to build than masonry dams, there were concerns about how it would hold up for the long haul. So several years later, a traditional masonry dam was constructed a mile upstream. If the steel dam failed, water would still be available for the railroad.

Turns out Francis Bainbridge knew his stuff. Only three steel dams were built in this country, and only the one he designed continues doing the job it was meant for. Both dams in Johnson Canyon still hold water, maintaining reservoirs that now provide recreational opportunities for visitors. A short hiking trail, known as the Stone to Steel Dam Trail, connects them. (928) 856-5600, www.fs.usda.gov/kaibab.

119. The first international airport of the Americas is found here.

In 1933, First Lady Eleanor Roosevelt dedicated the Douglas Airport as the first international airport in the Americas. The Douglas International

Airport was connected with the airfield in Agua Prieta, Mexico, by a north–south runway. Planes could land in Douglas then taxi into Mexico, and vice versa.

Douglas had other notable achievements in Arizona aviation history. In 1908, a few fearless guys built a glider using mail-order plans. The glider was pulled behind horses and launched by an aerial hitch. The next year they slapped a motor and propeller on their creation, the very first plane in Arizona.

Douglas was also one of the stops for the Women's Air Derby in 1929, the first official all-female air race in the United States. Dubbed the Powder Puff Derby by humorist Will Rogers, 19 women pilots took off from Santa Monica, California, and raced to Cleveland, Ohio. The distinguished roster of pilots included Pancho Barnes and Amelia Earhart.

120. The "Wickedest City in the West" was an Arizona mining camp.

By the turn of the 20th century, the Wild West already seemed a part of a fading past. But everyone forgot to tell the folks of Jerome. Clinging to the steep slopes of Cleopatra Hill, the mile-high boomtown was still running wide open with a rowdy mix of saloons, brothels, opium dens, and gunfights in the streets. In 1903, the *New York Sun* called Jerome "the wickedest town in the West."

Jerome's rowdy ways would continue for years to come.

121. Jerome is also the site of the most literal jailbreak in history.

While Jerome was populated with an all-star cast of desperadoes, it was actually the jailhouse that made a run for it. After some underground blasting in the 1930s, the concrete cellblock came unmoored and slid

Although a picturesque arts community today, Jerome had a wild and woolly past as a rowdy mining town. Courtesy of Mike Koopsen, Sedona.

down the steep hill, bumping across the landscape for more than 200 feet and landing in the middle of Hull Avenue, one of Jerome's main streets. "The road was altered to go around it," according to the historic plaque on site.

Eventually the Arizona Department of Transportation gave the fugitive jail another shove down the hill just to get it out of the road. It sits on a weedy slope secured now by an iron fence—bars for the bars—just in case it tries to run again.

122. The world's largest kaleidoscope store sits atop an Arizona hill.

Nellie Bly Kaleidoscopes, located in downtown Jerome, is the biggest brick-and-mortar kaleidoscope store in the world. They carry some cute

Nellie Bly Kaleidoscopes features handcrafted kaleidoscopes ranging from simple to elaborate. Courtesy of Mike Koopsen, Sedona.

little toy ones, but most of their color spinners are handmade by more than 90 artists and range in size, style, and price. They also have vintage scopes, acquired from private collections. Bring your good peeping eye and prepare to be dazzled.

Fill the object chamber of a kaleidoscope with just 10 pieces of glass, and they can arrange themselves into more than 3.5 million patterns. Scottish inventor David Brewster created the kaleidoscope back in 1816 and received a patent the following year. He was interested in the properties of light. 136 Main St., (928) 634-0255, www.nellieblyscopes.com.

123. Our insects changed the course of history.

Arizona teems with insects, menacing and strange, destructive and beautiful, but none scurried so dramatically across the pages of history like the cochineal.

The cochineal (*Dactylopius coccus*) belongs to a group of insects called scales. The females cluster on cactus pads, penetrate the plant with beak-like mouthparts, and feed on its juices. They secrete a white weblike substance for protection against the elements. And for several centuries they were considered as valuable as gold.

When Hernán Cortés landed in Mexico in 1519 he saw red. Literally. The Aztec men and women wore garments of a dazzling, vibrant crimson unlike anything existing in the Old World. Because it was the most difficult color to produce in a durable form, red signified wealth and social standing throughout Europe.

Witnessing the dyeing process, Cortés thought the pigment was ground from grain. But what he mistook for small gray seeds were actually baskets of dried insects. The cochineal he shipped back to Spain created an overwhelming demand. Europe's textile industry soon became dependent on cochineal, generating much needed revenue for the Spanish throne.

Producing a deep rich red that resists fading, the cochineal was so highly prized that its price was regularly quoted on the London and Amsterdam Commodity Exchanges. Michelangelo painted with this New World treasure, it adorned the robes of Roman Catholic cardinals, and the British Redcoats were marching advertisements. Without the cochineal Americans might be saluting the pink, white, and blue. It is suspected that Betsy Ross used colorfast cochineal dye when making the first US flag.

Newly hatched female cochineal move to a feeding spot and secrete long wax filaments. Later they crawl to the edge of the cactus pad where the wind catches the filaments and carries the cochineal to a new host. Males follow a different path. They pupate after hatching and then emerge as tiny, winged sex machines. The male cochineal stop eating as soon as they reach sexual maturity. They live for about a week doing nothing but flying among cacti copulating with as many females as possible. Then they die, presumably with a big smile.

Synthetic aniline dyes essentially replaced cochineal by the early 1900s. Yet with concerns about the safety of synthetic dyes, cochineal has experienced a comeback. Today, cochineal dye is used as coloring for cosmetics, medicines and foods—like yogurts, fruit juices, energy drinks, syrups, fillings, and soups. Look for cochineal or carmine on the label.

124. Tarantulas are hopeless romantics.

Despite starring in nightmares and old sci-fi movies, the big hairy spiders are willing to risk it all for love. Or at least sex. During the summer monsoon season, male tarantulas will leave their burrows in search of females. They risk being run over, or eaten by predators. They also risk a fate worse than death—the sting of a tarantula hawk, which is a large spider wasp, usually with blue-black bodies and orange wings. Their sting paralyzes the spider but does not kill it. The wasp then drags the helpless spider back to a burrow and lays a single egg. When the egg hatches, the larva chews into the tarantula's body and then chows down. All while the spider is still alive! Yikes!

But even if the tarantula survives all that and finds a female, there's a good chance she will kill him. Yet nothing deters him on his quest for love. Perhaps you'll regard tarantulas differently now.

FYI, tarantulas are venomous but are also quite docile. You would have to work hard at provoking the creature to bite, and even if they did, their venom is very mild and generally harmless for humans. The tarantula hawk, on the other hand, although not aggressive, delivers one of the most painful stings in the insect world.

125. The only movie where William Shatner costarred with 5,000 live tarantulas was filmed in Arizona.

Kingdom of the Spiders is a 1977 cult classic. It's one of those "nature on a rampage" flicks that became a horror subgenre in the 1970s. Filmed in the Verde Valley, Shatner was at his scenery-chewing best as a concerned yet macho veterinarian puzzled by mysterious deaths of local livestock. Spoiler alert: the big spiders are the villains. Turns out that hordes of tarantulas, their normal food supply eradicated by pesticides, have banded together to bring down bigger game.

A big chunk of the film's budget went for the purchase of live tarantulas. The crew put out word they were paying $10 apiece for the spiders, and locals collected 5,000 of them. Which also caused some problems because each tarantula demanded their own trailer. Sort of. They had to be kept warm and separated from each other. Also, since tarantulas are naturally shy, fans had to be used—as well as general prodding—to get them to move toward the thing they were supposed to be attacking. In most scenes, the spiders seem to just be milling about while their human costars run around screaming.

To increase the horror factor, the film crew painted thousands of spiders on buildings in downtown Camp Verde. After the production wrapped, they repainted. But for years afterward as that hastily applied top coat faded, the dark outlines of the tarantulas could be seen on buildings all over town.

126. The Gila monster is the only venomous lizard in the United States.

Another star of sci-fi flicks, Gila monsters are large heavy-bodied lizards, brightly colored with beaded skin and black eyes. Lifeless eyes, like a doll's eyes, if you want to get all Captain Quint about it. (A remake of *Jaws* with Gila monsters instead of sharks has blockbuster written all over it!)

Gilas are desert dwellers living near arroyos and rocky foothills. Primarily found in Arizona and Mexico, their range extends to isolated corners in surrounding states. They are the largest lizards native to this country.

While a Gila monster bite can be quite painful, they have never resulted in a human death. Courtesy of Rick Mortensen, Cincinnati.

Don't be lulled by their sluggish movements, Gilas can strike with surprising speed. Using large grooved teeth in their lower jaw, they clamp on and chew their venom into the wound. Although a Gila monster bite can be extremely painful, none has resulted in a reported human death.

Unlike rattlesnakes, Gilas don't use their venom to kill their prey. They let their size and powerful jaws handle their business. The poison saliva is just something to deter predators and dim-witted humans who are somehow not dissuaded by the fact that the word *MONSTER* is in their name as they reach down to handle the beasts.

127. Sierra Vista is the Hummingbird Capital of the United States.

The official title is "Hummingbird Capital of Arizona" as decreed by the governor. But that's only because his powers don't extend beyond the border. More species of the colorful little winged jewels have been recorded in Arizona than any other state, except maybe Texas. Bird-watchers have spotted 15 in Sierra Vista alone, located in the southeastern corner of the state, our birding hot spot. Number 15, the purple-throated Lucifer, is pretty rare, but 14 different species are commonly seen. That's a lot of wee flyers buzzing around feeders and flower beds. And if you're going to be overrun by something, what's cuter than an infestation of hummingbirds?

128. People travel from all over the world to admire our birds.

Important Birding Areas (IBA) can be found all over Arizona, but there's an especially high concentration amid the Sky Islands of the southeastern corner of the state. The Arizona species list of around 550 is the highest of any state without an ocean coastline. Only California and Texas can claim more. This is the northern edge of the range of several visitors that occasionally cross the border from Mexico, like the elegant trogon, and that generates all sorts of excitement.

Arizona is also known as a release site for the endangered California condor, the largest flying land bird in North America with a massive wingspan of up to 9.5 feet. In 1982, only 22 condors were left in the world. A captive breeding program was initiated, and in 1996 the

first six birds were released at Arizona's Vermilion Cliffs. In 2003, we celebrated

A California condor glides above the Grand Canyon. Courtesy of Mike Koopsen, Sedona.

the fledging of a wild condor chick, the first in the state in more than 100 years.

More releases have led to a growing population of the giant birds. Each condor is outfitted with a radio transmitter and numbered wing tags so biologists can monitor them. California condors are most often seen around the Vermilion Cliffs and at the Grand Canyon, where they love riding the thermal updrafts. They can soar and glide up to 50 miles per hour.

129. Roadrunners are more than just turbocharged cartoon masterminds.

The lanky birds are real. Coyotes wearing rocket-powered roller skates are less common.

While certainly not exclusive to Arizona, the distinctive-looking roadrunner just looks perfectly at home sprinting through the saguaros of the Sonoran Desert. Part of the cuckoo family, they're large ground birds with long tails, an expressive head crest, and some serious wheels. They can reach speeds of 25 miles per hour. Roadrunners can fly for short distances but don't seem to enjoy it.

The birds are also bad hombres to tangle with. They'll eat just about anything they can catch. That includes rattlesnakes. Sometimes they will grab the rattler and bash its head against the ground to kill it. Other times they peck through the back of its head. Then the bird swallows the snake whole. Now that's something you don't see in the cartoons.

Unlike their cartoon counterpart, real roadrunners don't say "beep beep" or "meep meep" or anything like that. Courtesy of Mike Koopsen, Sedona.

130. There would be no Arizona if not for a certain feisty fashionista.

If not for Sharlot Madbrith Hall, we would have been just a misshapen New Mexico appendage. In 1905 President Teddy Roosevelt recommended that the territories of New Mexico and Arizona be admitted to the union as a single state. Adamantly opposed to the notion, Sharlot Hall penned a poem called "Arizona" celebrating the beauty of the territory. The poem was published in newspapers across the land, and was sent to every member of Congress. It sparked a rallying cry against the plan. The bill passed through the House of Representatives, but before the Senate approved it the language for joint statehood was removed.

In 1909, Hall was appointed Territorial Historian, becoming the first Arizona woman to hold public office. She saw the need to preserve Arizona's history and began collecting a wealth of Native American and pioneer material. In 1911, Hall made a lengthy trek across the Arizona Strip to raise awareness of its potential and to prevent Utah from acquiring the lonely land.

When Arizona achieved statehood in 1912, Hall's position was eliminated. Hall took some time to care for her aging parents but continued to write and stayed active in politics. After Calvin Coolidge became president, Hall was chosen as the elector to deliver Arizona's three electoral votes in Washington. For the occasion, she wore a special custom gown made of copper. The dress weighed 9 pounds. Afterward, Hall would attend special functions in Prescott wearing the metal dress along with a hat made from cactus.

She secured a lease on the first Territorial Governor's Mansion in Prescott, restored the building, and stocked it with her extensive collection of artifacts. It opened in 1928. After Hall's death in 1943, a historical society continued her efforts. Today, the Governor's Mansion serves as the centerpiece for a sprawling museum campus not far from Prescott's Courthouse

Plaza. It includes historic buildings, heritage gardens, and compelling exhibits and is known as the Sharlot Hall Museum. 415 W. Gurley St., (928) 445-3122, www.sharlothallmuseum.org.

131. Sun City was the first 55-plus active adult retirement community in the country.

Del Webb built it in 1960. Do some residents still cruise around town in golf carts? Absolutely. Know why? Because they can.

132. Fictional trees grow at Boyce Thompson Arboretum.

Tucked away in Arizona's largest arboretum, amid an amazing collection of arid-loving plants, grows the freakish boojum tree. Found only in the deserts of Baja California and Sonora, Mexico, the boojum looks like a spiny upside-down and out-of-control carrot. The stiff upward-tapering trunk bristles with short slender branches and small leaves that generally drop off during warm weather. They're related to ocotillos but are definitely the black sheep of the family. Naturalist Godfrey Sykes of the Desert Laboratory in Tucson bestowed the boojum name on the curious plants. It comes from the mythical Boojum featured in Lewis Carroll's poem *The Hunting of the Snark.*

Other boojums can be found in the Desert Botanical Garden in Phoenix and the University of Arizona Campus Krutch Garden.

133. America's most famous missing gold mine is somewhere in the Superstition Mountains.

Or maybe not. It all depends on whether you believe the story of the Lost Dutchman Mine. The Dutchman in question was actually a German immigrant named Jacob Waltz. While there are many variations of the

The Lost Dutchman Mine is a legend that has lured many to their deaths in the past century. Photo by the author.

story, they all revolve around the notion that Waltz discovered a wealthy gold mine in the 1870s—one that may have belonged to the Peralta family of Mexico. Or perhaps it was a cache of gold hidden by Apaches.

Waltz made many trips into the rugged Superstitions, a land of sheer cliffs and slashing canyons, to retrieve gold as needed. Finally, while on his deathbed in 1891, he described the location of the mine to a neighbor who was caring for him. Even though she soon set out in search of the treasure, she never found it. When her quest proved unsuccessful, she began selling maps and clues to the mine.

The legend of the Lost Dutchman Mine took a more sinister turn in the 1930s. In June 1931, Adolph Ruth, a retired government worker and amateur treasure hunter, ventured into the Superstition Mountains. Armed with maps and years of research, Ruth felt certain he could find the elusive mine. He was never seen alive again. Six months later searchers found his skull punctured with what appeared to be two large bullet holes.

More deaths would follow. Despite the fact that no geological evidence indicates a gold mine could exist within the fractured volcanic fortress of the Superstitions, thousands of folks have sought Jacob Waltz's fabled treasure. Dozens, perhaps hundreds, have perished in the unforgiving terrain. In July 2010, three Utah hikers decided to scout around in the backcountry searching for clues. Their remains were found a few months later. The Lost Dutchman Mine remains a tantalizing and deadly mystery.

134. Arizona has the largest private museum dedicated to the American Indian experience.

The Heard Museum is one of the world's foremost museums celebrating Native American culture and art. From extremely modest beginnings—it was started in 1929 to house the collection of its founders—the Phoenix museum has continued to grow and receives international acclaim for its collection of more than 40,000 pieces of Native American artifacts and artwork. This place gives a contemporary voice to Native cultures. Along with the permanent exhibits, family-friendly interactive projects, and the extensive library, the museum also features the American Indian Veterans National Memorial, honoring those who have served. It is the only such monument in the United States.

The Heard hosts several annual gatherings and events showcasing art, dance, and culture that draw huge crowds. The museum shop is filled with an array of striking, authentic work. Here you'll find jewelry, pottery, textiles, carvings, paintings, and more. The majority of pieces in the inventory are purchased directly from the artists. 2301 N. Central Ave., (602) 252-8840, www.heard.org.

135. Famed architect Frank Lloyd Wright was one of the earliest snowbirds.

Tired of bleak Wisconsin winters, Frank Lloyd Wright came to Scottsdale in 1937 and built his winter home. Taliesin West also served as the main campus for the Frank Lloyd Wright School of Architecture. The complex drew its name from Taliesin, his digs in Spring Green, Wisconsin.

Spread across the foothills of the McDowell Mountains in Scottsdale, Taliesin West highlights several of Wright's design principles. He believed that structures should not intrude on their environment but should seem to grow from it, and that all the components appear unified. The clustered buildings mirror the shapes and colors of the rugged desert that Wright found so intriguing. Using local stone and low profiles, and integrating indoor and outdoor spaces, the enclave coexists harmoniously with its surroundings. Dramatic terraces, gardens, and walkways link many of the buildings. Today, the National Historic Landmark houses the Frank Lloyd Wright Foundation and offers public tours. In 2019, Taliesin West and seven other properties were designated as a UNESCO World Heritage Site under the title "The 20th-Century Architecture of Frank Lloyd Wright." 12621 N. Frank Lloyd Wright Blvd., (480) 860-2700, www.franklloydwright.org.

136. Arizona's natural architecture inspires legendary architects.

Italian architect Paolo Soleri came to Arizona to study under Frank Lloyd Wright. Although the two men clashed over differing visions, they did share an interest in incorporating natural elements into their designs. Soleri settled in farmland north of Phoenix in 1955, building Cosanti, his architectural and design studio in Paradise Valley.

This is where Soleri first began using his trademark earth-casting

Cosanti, designed by Paolo Soleri, still sells the famous wind-bells and offers tours of the grounds. Photo by the author.

technique, a process that involves pouring concrete over river-silt molds. Once the concrete hardens, the earth is removed, leaving the hollow forms. South-facing half-domes, known as apses, create year-round workspaces as they provide summer shade while embracing winter sun. Many of the structures are partially underground for insulation. Set amid garden paths and terraced beds, Cosanti maintains an artistic ethereal feel, enhanced by the musical cascades of Soleri's famous wind-bells. Cosanti still sells the bronze and ceramic bells and offers tours of the grounds. 6433 E. Doubletree Ranch Rd., (480) 948-6145, www.cosanti.com.

While Frank Lloyd Wright advocated single-family homes and

suburban development, Soleri believed that was wasteful and created a dependence on automobiles. He felt urban habitats should be compact, efficient, and sensitive to the environment. He coined the term "arcology" to describe the concept of architecture shaped by ecology to create a more sustainable lifestyle. That's what inspired him to begin work at Arcosanti in the high desert of Cordes Junction.

Arcosanti looks like a Dr. Seuss construction site, consisting of a series of structures both striking and fanciful. Clustered modular residences, large circular windows, and curving rooflines rise above a dry riverbed. Soleri broke ground on Arcosanti in 1970.

The idea of Arcosanti is that 5,000 people could live within a largely self-sustaining community perched on a mere 25 acres. Everything would be within walking distance and surrounded by a large swath of pristine desert. It hasn't quite panned out as only a fraction of the futuristic city has been built thus far. Soleri died in 2013, but his followers keep Arcosanti going. Today it serves primarily as a learning institution.

General tours of Arcosanti are offered daily. These tours provide a look at the history, design, and functionality of the project, and you'll often get to see the famous Soleri wind-bells being cast in the foundry. Workshops, ranging from single day to multi-week, are also available. The café serves simple healthy meals and homemade baked goods. Overnight accommodations are available by reservation. www.arcosanti.org.

137. Most of pioneering architect Mary Colter's surviving properties are found in Arizona.

While the Grand Canyon would be spectacular even if Mary Colter hadn't showed up, it would be a very different experience for travelers. Architect Mary Elizabeth Jane Colter was America's most influential

Desert View Watchtower at the eastern edge of Grand Canyon National Park is one of Mary Colter's signature designs. Courtesy of Mike Koopsen, Sedona.

female designer who revolutionized Southwest construction. And the bulk of Colter's surviving work can be found in Arizona.

Colter was hired by the Fred Harvey Company to design hotels, restaurants, and gift shops along the Santa Fe Railway. In 1904, she built Hopi House, a gift shop and cultural center next to the El Tovar Hotel at the South Rim of the Grand Canyon. But while the stately El Tovar borrows styles from Swiss chalets and Norwegian villas, Colter's structure looks as if it has perched there for centuries. The multiple stepped roofs, small windows, low doorways, and thatched ceilings, all slightly uneven, give the impression of pueblo architecture, ancient and Indigenous. Colter went on to build many of the notable Grand Canyon structures like

Bright Angel Lodge, Lookout Studio, Desert View Watchtower, Hermit's Rest, and Phantom Ranch.

At the time, European ideas still held considerable sway over architectural styles in the United States. Colter pushed things in a drastically different direction with her use of site materials and her efforts to create buildings harmonious to their natural setting. She laid out the blueprint for National Park Service structures. Her style became known as National Park Rustic and can be seen in parks throughout the West.

Colter's masterpiece was La Posada in Winslow, the last great railroad hotel. Built in 1930, the opulent Spanish-style hacienda was the only project for which Colter designed the buildings, decorated the interiors, and planted the gardens. She oversaw every detail, right down to the china patterns and the maids' uniforms. After being closed for decades, La Posada has been restored to its original splendor and again welcomes guests. 303 E. Second Street, (928) 289-4366, www.laposada.org.

138. America's oldest, longest, and maybe fastest coaster race burns up an Arizona road.

It's a July 4 tradition in Bisbee. Groups of speed-crazed kids go careening down the hills and around the steep curves of Tombstone Canyon in sleek hand-built coasters. The Bisbee Coaster Race started in 1914, harkening back to the town's mining days. It's the oldest, longest, and probably fastest gravity-powered vehicle race in the country. The competition has a bit of a checkered past, with adults horning in on the action for a time. Grown-up drivers meant heavier cars and greater speeds, leading to serious accidents in the 1950s and again in 1980. Since 1993 coaster racing is strictly for the youngsters. Kids ages 9 to 16 compete for prizes while spectators line the 3-mile course that rolls right through the heart of historic downtown Bisbee.

139. The most dangerous animal in the Grand Canyon is also its most adorable.

Despite being home to six species of rattlesnake, the most dangerous creature at Grand Canyon is the cute and furry rock squirrel. Dozens of people each year are bitten, most while attempting to feed the squirrels or take selfies with them. The old axiom about not biting the hand that feeds you does not translate to rock squirrels. They have absolutely no qualms about sinking their sharp little nut-cracking teeth into your soft flesh, snatching proffered snacks, and then disappearing into the woods.

While rock squirrels often gather near high-traffic areas hoping to score handouts, just ignore them and keep your distance. They're not actually cuddly. Do not feed them, and do not try to take a selfie with them. You're at the Grand Canyon—you should be able to find something besides rodents to photograph.

140. Arizona prompted one of the worst predictions in history.

In 1857, Lieutenant Joseph Christmas Ives took a shallow-draft steamboat up the Colorado River as part of a military survey expedition. When it crashed below the current site of Hoover Dam, he continued upriver on a skiff, at last proceeding on foot. The determined lieutenant is credited with being the first European American to reach the river within the Grand Canyon.

Yet what Ives wrote defined him for all time as the Anti-Nostradamus. Part of his chronicles had this to say about the Grand Canyon: "The region is, of course, altogether valueless. It can be approached only from the south, and after entering it there is nothing to do but leave. Ours has been the first, and will doubtless be the last, party of whites to visit this profitless locality."

Surprisingly, Lt. Joseph Christmas Ives was mistaken in his assessment that no one else would be interested in visiting the Grand Canyon. Courtesy of Mike Koopsen, Sedona.

141. The first instant photography business in history began on the edge of the Grand Canyon.

Ellsworth Kolb and Emery Kolb set up a photography business on the South Rim of the Grand Canyon in 1903. It would make them world famous thanks to their talent, persistence, and sturdy leg muscles.

The young brothers lived and worked out of a tent situated at the head of the Bright Angel Trail, which was the Bright Angel Toll Road at the time. The Kolbs would collect the toll from mule riders about to start down into the depths and then snap photos. One of the brothers (usually Emery) would load the glass-plate negatives into a pack, and race down the trail. The photographer soon passed the mule train, and kept running down the switchbacks, dropping 3,000 feet in elevation for a total length of 4.6 miles to the shady oasis of Indian Garden. Since this was the nearest clean water, the Kolbs built a darkroom here.

Emery (or Ellsworth) would wash the plates, develop the photographs, load them back into the pack, and start running back toward the rim. This time it was all uphill, through dozens of switchbacks, a 3,000-foot elevation gain, and 4.6 miles of trail—a 9.2-mile round trip. And the brothers would be standing at the rim with new photos ready to sell when the mule riders emerged from the canyon. Oh yeah, they often did this twice a day.

Decades before Polaroid released its first instant camera, two young guys had already invented the instant photography business in Arizona.

142. The ultimate bucket-list hike is an Arizona classic.

Tell someone you're hiking rim-to-rim and they don't have to ask where. Anyone who owns a pair of hiking boots has at least dreamed of venturing across the Grand Canyon on foot, traveling from one rim to the other. When you have a chance to walk through one of the Seven Natural Wonders of the World, you just don't pass that up.

Most people start from the lonelier North Rim. It rises 1,000 feet higher than the South Rim so that's 1,000 feet you don't have to climb. North Rim is only open from May 15 through October 15, so there's the window to plan your adventure. The grueling trek stretches for nearly 24 miles descending on the North Kaibab Trail and climbing out on Bright Angel Trail. Inner canyon temperatures can be scorching, the elevation can be challenging, and the hike, exhausting. Yet it is the kind of singular experience that has the power to transform lives.

Do not take this hike lightly. Research, train, prepare. It can be done in a single day by hikers who are extremely fit and fast. Although the National Park Service strongly discourages that. Hundreds of people have to be rescued from the canyon each year, and some don't survive. It's best to spend a night or two under the rim and make the time last. There are three campgrounds along the route (Cottonwood, Bright

Every Grand Canyon hike is an adventure, but going rim-to-rim is downright epic. Courtesy of Mike Koopsen, Sedona.

Angel, and Indian Garden), and all require a backcountry permit that must be secured in advance.

I think the best way to tackle the hike is to score a bed at Phantom Ranch. That way you only have to carry a daypack. Of course, landing a cabin or a dorm bed at Phantom is not easy. It involves entering a lottery system to try and secure a spot 13 months in advance. Start with that, and then you've got a year to get in shape and sort out all the other logistics like rim lodging and a trans-canyon shuttle since a 215-mile drive separates the two rims. And to eagerly anticipate the adventure of a lifetime.

143. Another of our hikes is so mind-bendingly gorgeous, it requires a lottery to keep it from being overrun.

The Wave is an exotic sandstone bowl laced with ribbons of swirling strata that feels like you're crossing the surface of a distant and dreamy

After securing an elusive permit, reaching the Wave requires a strenuous 6.4-mile round-trip hike. Courtesy of Mike Koopsen, Sedona.

planet. Located in the Vermilion Cliffs National Monument, it has become a much sought-after destination in the era of social media feeds. Permits are required and extremely difficult to come by. Once you've secured a permit, expect a moderately difficult and poorly marked hike of just over 3 miles across sand and sandstone to reach the Wave.

To protect the delicate sandstone structure, the Bureau of Land Management limits access to only 16 groups (no more than 64 people) per day. Of those, 48 people or 12 groups (whichever comes first) are chosen in an online lottery 4 months in advance. The other option is to sign up for a Daily Lottery. Permits are issued 2 days in advance, but you can only apply on a mobile device within a geofenced area in Northern Arizona / Southern Utah. BLM Field Office Kanab, Utah: (435) 688-3200, blm.gov/visit/kanab-visitor-center.

144. Arizona has the only Pony Express that still delivers mail for the US Postal Service.

Every winter horseback riders gallop across the high plains of northern Arizona, through pine forests, down the Mogollon Rim, over the rugged Mazatzal Mountains, and between the tall saguaros of the Sonoran Desert—all to deliver the mail.

The Hashknife Pony Express keeps the romance of the Old West alive. Each January/February, more than two dozen riders carry the mail, relaying the big canvas bags along the route, which stretches for more than 200 miles from Holbrook to Scottsdale.

They deliver about 20,000 pieces of first-class mail annually. All letters are hand stamped with the official ride logo, the highly coveted cachet sought by stamp collectors everywhere. The Hashknife is the oldest Pony Express sanctioned by the US Postal Service. Each rider is sworn in as an honorary mail messenger before setting out on the rigorous 3-day journey.

The "hashknife" was the tool once used by chuck wagon cooks to cut beef and vegetables for hash to feed hungry cowboys. The Aztec Land and Cattle Company adopted the Hashknife brand and moved from Texas to Holbrook in 1866. They quickly developed a reputation as a rough and rowdy bunch, not above a little rustling or stagecoach robbing. In 1957, the Navajo County Sheriff's Posse retained limited use of the brand, and it identifies the Pony Express. All riders are members of the Navajo County Sheriff's Posse or their guests. The arrival of the Hashknife Pony Express in Scottsdale kicks off the annual Parada del Sol, celebrating the town's rich multicultural history. www.hashknifeponyexpress.com.

145. In Arizona you can dine in America's most remote restaurant.

A collection of rustic cabins and dorms are scattered beneath the cottonwood trees at the bottom of the Grand Canyon on the north side of the Colorado River. Designed by architect Mary Colter, Phantom Ranch is the only place in the national park where visitors can actually sleep in a bed below the rim. Nestled on the banks of Bright Angel Creek, the little outpost is a welcome oasis for weary hikers and mule riders.

At the heart of the complex is the Phantom Ranch Canteen, an exclusive joint if there ever was one. Since parking is extremely tricky, customers arrive via a long, grueling but heart-squeezing hike on one of the canyon's three corridor trails. It's 14 miles down the North Kaibab Trail to Phantom Ranch, 9.6 miles down the Bright Angel, or 7.8 miles on the shadeless South Kaibab. And that's the easy part. You still have to hike back out after your meal, and it's uphill all the way.

Yet almost as challenging as the walk from the parking lot is securing a reservation. You can't just show up waving a fiver at the host hoping to snag a seat. Everything at Phantom Ranch requires reservations. If you want a bed in a cabin or dorm, it means entering an online lottery that accepts entries 13 months in advance. Book your meal reservations at the same time. Overnight mule rides to Phantom Ranch include accommodations and meals. Breakfast and dinner at the canteen are served family style on long communal tables. Simple food but well prepared.

Sometimes rim-to-rim hikers, river rafters, or backpackers at the nearby Bright Angel Campground reserve meals. Sack lunches to go are also offered. During limited hours, the canteen is open to the public and sells a few supplies, snacks, and cold drinks. Trust me when

The Phantom Ranch Canteen at the bottom of the Grand Canyon may be America's most remote and exclusive eatery. Courtesy of Mike Koopsen, Sedona.

I say, after hiking from the rim to the river in the sizzling summer heat, with a hike out still looming, an ice-cold lemonade tastes heaven-sent. (888) 297-2757, www.grandcanyonlodges.com.

146. Tucson was the first American city to be named a UNESCO City of Gastronomy.

The United Nations Educational, Scientific and Cultural Organization (UNESCO) recognized Tucson for its active food and agricultural efforts today as well as its cultural farming and food heritage.

According to UNESCO, Tucson has the "longest agricultural history of any city in the United States." Evidence of cultivation in the area dates back 4,000 years. It has a 300-year tradition of vineyards, orchards, and livestock ranching. A long-standing framework of sustainable techniques and local food production and distribution is evident in the numerous farmers markets, cultural celebrations, festivals, and thriving culinary scene.

147. The nation's oldest Mexican restaurant in continuous operation by the same family is in Tucson.

Monica Flin opened El Charro Café in 1922. While women-owned businesses were not common at the time, her passion and hard work kept the restaurant going. She came to Tucson from France in the 1800s when her father, Jules, a stonemason, was commissioned to build the city's St. Augustine Chapel. Jules also built the family home on Court Street in 1896. When Monica inherited the mission-style building, she moved her small restaurant into the larger space, and it has been there ever since.

El Charro has stayed in the family and has won countless accolades over the decades. They are famous for their carne seca, strips of thin-sliced beef marinated in garlic and lemon juice, then air-dried in cages by the hot desert sun. After being shredded, the succulent meat is added to dishes ranging from tacos to enchiladas to chimichangas. In recent years, additional El Charro locations have opened around Tucson. www.elcharrocafe.com.

148. The chimichanga was invented in Arizona.

There's still a little debate about who invented the chimichanga. But what's in general agreement is that it happened in Arizona. For the uninitiated, the chimi is a burrito that crosses over to the dark side. It starts out as a large flour tortilla filled with a choice of meat, vegetables, and spices, all rolled up, just like a burrito. Then it takes a turn. The concoction is deep-fried to golden perfection and served on a plate, all hot and crunchy and savory. You can have them with or without sauce, or with other toppings like sour cream and guacamole.

There are origin stories at a few Arizona restaurants, but it generally comes down to two main contenders. Woody Johnson, owner of Macayo's in Phoenix, claims to have invented the chimi in the late 1940s when he wanted to repurpose a batch of day-old burritos and decided the best way to do that involved a dip in the deep fryer.

But the woman often regarded as the creator of the dish is Monica Flin of El Charro in Tucson. Legend has it that she accidentally dropped a burrito in a deep fryer, splattering oil everywhere. Since children were nearby, a stifled curse word was quickly changed to "chimichanga," a slang term that basically means "thingamajig."

149. We introduced America to the Sonoran hot dog. You're welcome.

The Sonoran hot dog is the saguaro cactus of wieners, an Arizona icon. While the messy concoction originated in Hermosillo, Sonora, it exploded on this side of the border in Tucson. One of the men responsible for the widespread popularity of the Sonoran dog is Daniel Contreras, who started El Guero Canelo in 1993. What began as a food cart has grown into multiple restaurants and a coveted James Beard Award. For a hot dog! Yes, it's that delicious. www.elguerocanelo.com.

The Sonoran is a special kind of sin, a hot dog wrapped snug in bacon and then grilled, fusing the meats into a smoky flavor bomb. It is then tucked into a soft boat of dough called a bolillo, a split-top roll fluffier and sweeter than traditional buns and closed at the ends to contain the avalanche of additional ingredients. Piled around the bacon-swaddled dog are whole pinto beans, diced tomatoes, grilled and fresh onions, mustard, mayo, and jalapeño sauce.

The decadently delicious Sonoran hot dog is Arizona's unofficial state wiener. Photo by the author.

This is what the borderlands taste like, that casual blending of cultures and flavors. The all-American hot dog gets a Mexican makeover. This is folk art. This is street music. Every bite unleashes a spicy, smoky, salty, creamy crescendo. The offhand elegance of the dish takes you by surprise and rocks you back on your heels as you ponder the years you've wasted shoving less complex wieners in your face. You begin craving another before you're halfway through the first one. It will cure a hangover, mend a broken heart, and raise your self-esteem. The Sonoran hot dog is the reason why food carts and taco trucks exist. The memory of your first leaves a permanent tattoo on your taste buds. Try one, and you'll know you're in Arizona.

Of course, I always get my Sonoran hot dog without mayo, which I consider to be the devil's ointment.

150. Pope Leo XIII was responsible for Tucson's nickname, the "Old Pueblo."

Politicians are politicians no matter the century. In 1880, when the railroad first arrived in Tucson, Mayor R. N. "Bob" Leatherwood couldn't help but crow a little. He fired off telegrams to the mayors of Los Angeles and San Francisco, President Rutherford B. Hayes, and Pope Leo XIII. Leatherwood's telegram to the pope said:

"The mayor of Tucson begs the honor of reminding Your Holiness that this ancient and honorable pueblo was founded by the Spaniards under the sanction of the church more than three centuries ago, and to inform Your Holiness that a railroad from San Francisco, California, now connects us with the Christian World."

Reporters got quite a kick out of the mayor helloing the pope. And "ancient and honorable pueblo" had a nice ring to it. After a while it began appearing in newspapers as the "A. and H. Pueblo," which eventually morphed into the "Old Pueblo." By the 1920s, Old Pueblo became a regular slogan in ads aimed at Eastern tourists, branding Tucson with a rich Spanish–Indian flavor. And it's been the Old Pueblo ever since.

151. Ray Bradbury launched his career in Tucson.

The celebrated author and man most responsible for bringing science fiction into the literary mainstream began pursuing his passion as a 12-year-old kid living in Tucson. His neighbor's collection of pulp science fiction sparked a fascination with giant insects, otherworld creatures, and ray-gun-packing spacemen. That's when he began pounding out his own stories on a $6 typewriter, sequels to ones he read.

"I've always had a very special love for Tucson," he told the *Arizona Daily Star*. "It was while I lived here that I decided where I wanted to go. I've gone there and I've gone beyond."

It was also in Tucson where Bradbury turned professional, landing a gig on KGAR radio. He would read the newspaper comic strips over the air on Saturday nights, changing voices with each character. He did that for about 5 months, recalling fondly, "And my pay was free tickets to see *King Kong, Murders in the Wax Museum,* and *The Mummy.* You

The San Pedro Riparian National Conservation Area provides critical habitat for wildlife in southern Arizona. Photo by the author.

can't do any better than that. I've never had better income in my life since."

152. Only two places in the country are designated as Riparian National Conservation Areas, and both are in southern Arizona.

The Bureau of Land Management oversees 17 National Conservation Areas and 6 similarly designated parcels in 10 states. These lands offer exceptional scientific, cultural, ecological, historical, and recreational value. Yet only 2 are known as Riparian National Conservation Areas, preserving vital waterways, and they're both found in arid, desert-intensive Arizona. Weird, huh?

The San Pedro Riparian National Conservation Area protects a 40-mile stretch of the San Pedro River between the Mexican border and the town of St. David. The river nourishes a slender forest of cottonwood and willow trees, and creates some of the richest wildlife habitat in the Southwest. The San Pedro supports more than 350 species of birds and 80-plus mammals.

The Gila Box Riparian National Conservation Area covers 23,000 acres of rugged terrain fed by four perennial waterways: Gila River, Bonito Creek, Eagle Creek, and San Francisco River. Northeast of Safford, Gila Box is an isolated area of cliffs and canyons, primitive roads, and winding trails. It's an easy place to fall off the grid for a while. Bighorn sheep are often spotted here.

153. San Francisco was actually settled by Arizonans.

During Spanish Colonial times, Juan Bautista de Anza served as captain of the Tubac Presidio, the first European settlement in Arizona. A respected soldier and leader, Anza was also an explorer. In 1774 he established an overland route to Alta California, traveling through the Sonoran Desert to reach the Pacific Coast. Eager to expand Spanish territory, Anza organized a colonizing expedition the very next year.

Anza and his traveling village consisted of 240 soldiers and settlers, and 1,000 head of livestock. They set out in October 1775. The 5-month journey took them to the San Francisco Bay, where they established a presidio and mission, forming the city where Tony Bennett would later leave his heart.

154. In Douglas, you'll find the only place in the world with four churches on the four corners of the same block.

There's nothing else on the block located between 10th Street and 11th Street, and D Avenue and E Avenue. It's just the four prayer palaces.

Holding down the corners of Church Square are Southern Baptist, Presbyterian, Episcopal, and Methodist.

155. The only US nuclear missile silo open to the public is found south of Tucson.

Titan Missile Museum is a haunting spot, a relic of a tense time that, sadly, never seems as distant as it should be. On alert from 1963 to 1987, the Titan II carried the largest nuclear warhead ever deployed, with a range of 5,500 miles. There were 54 of the big nukes locked and loaded with each site staffed around the clock by a four-person missile combat crew for 24-hour shifts. All the missiles were eventually deactivated, and this is the only Titan II site left intact. Located in Sahuarita just south of Tucson, visitors climb into a silo to examine the actual Titan II missile still resting on its launch pad and looking as quietly ferocious as ever.

Guided tours are offered daily, showing off the missile complex, launch center, 3-ton blast doors, and a close look at the largest nuke ever made in the United States. A simulated launch is conducted complete with secret codes, two-key ignition, and countdown. The missile is unarmed, so you don't have to worry about your rambunctious youngster bumping a button and accidentally starting World War III. 1580 W. Duval Mine Rd., (520) 625-7736, www.titanmissilemuseum.org.

156. Arizona maintains the largest aircraft boneyard in the world.

The 309th Aerospace Maintenance and Regeneration Group (AMARG) takes care of nearly 4,000 aircraft, making it the largest aircraft storage and preservation facility in the world. Located at Davis-Monthan Air Force Base in Tucson, the facility has been building its impressive collection since the end of World War II.

Among the first planes received were B-29 bombers—critical for the war but not needed in peacetime. In recent years the 309th AMARG, known as the Boneyard, has become the sole repository of out-of-service aircraft from all branches of the US government. Dry desert air and limited rainfall provide the perfect environment for the 309th AMARG, and the hard soil surface keeps the aircraft from sinking into the ground.

Yet Boneyard doesn't mean graveyard. The aircraft are carefully maintained, and many of the planes at the Boneyard emerge from retirement to fly again. Some are used to recycle parts, which helps keep other planes modernized and in the air. To visit the Boneyard, take one of the bus tours offered from the adjacent Pima Air & Space Museum, which is the largest privately funded aviation and aerospace museum in the country, and the third-largest aviation museum in the world. (520) 574-0462, www.pimaair.org.

157. At the other end of the spectrum, we have the world's largest collection of handmade miniature airplanes.

Comprised of 5,825 wooden airplanes and other flying machines, the Kalusa Collection is housed in the Hazy Library at Embry-Riddle Aeronautical University in Prescott. Each plane is built to a precise scale of one-eighteenth of an inch to a foot. Consistent use of the scale means all aircraft in the collection maintain accurate size relations to one another.

John W. Kalusa began making World War I models in 1936 at the age of 14. After serving as an aerial photographer and mechanic in World War II, he resumed his hobby. Each model is painted with the detailed markings characteristic of the aircraft. Kalusa carved and painted an average of two models per week right up until his death in 2003. His work was recognized as the world's largest collection of handmade air-planes by the Guinness Book of World Records.

158. Arizona is the Dwarf Car Capital of the world.

And it's all because of one man. Ernie Adams is known as "Mr. Dwarf Car." Adams creates one-of-a-kind masterpieces, tiny duplicates of classic automobiles. They are on an eleven-sixteenths scale, and except for the engine and transmission every part of the car is hand built, including frame, body, suspension, bumpers, grille, instruments, door handles, and trim.

Adams holds court in the Dwarf Car Museum in Maricopa, an hour south of Phoenix. Inside the barnlike structure it looks like your average garage. Tools are out, projects are ongoing, a vintage soda machine sits in the corner, and walls are adorned with old signs and memorabilia. The only difference is that the dozen classic cars

Ernie Adams poses with his hand-built Dwarf '42 Ford Deluxe convertible, a car that he's driven across the country. Photo by the author.

lining the garage are distinctly undersized, standing about 46 inches in height. Despite their Muppet Baby adorableness, these are fully functioning street legal automobiles.

Adams crafted the first Dwarf car in 1965, a replica of a 1928 Chevy 2-door sedan, using crude tools and the steel from nine refrigerators. Equipped with a 2-cylinder, 13-horsepower Onan motor, the first Dwarf car is still driven today.

It was Adams who started the Dwarf Car Racing phenomenon. He built the first Dwarf race car. His friend Daren Schmaltz soon built another. The vehicles were steel-bodied, powered by motorcycle engines, and were an instant hit in the first race at the 1983 Yavapai County Fair. But after a few years, Adams left the sport to focus on building fully dressed Dwarf cruisers with fenders, chrome, and finished interiors.

During years of building Dwarf racers, Adams sharpened his skill at bending and shaping metal. He works with a large homemade English wheel that enables him to make compound curves. His Dwarf cruisers are virtually indistinguishable from their normal-sized counterparts.

His Dwarf '42 Ford Deluxe convertible includes a fabricated hydraulic convertible top that is fully operational. He has driven the little Ford cross-country participating in car shows. A '49 Mercury includes baby moon hubcaps, fender skirts, and two spotlights. The car is nosed and decked (chrome trim removed from the hood and trunk) and sports a Fulton-style sun visor. His '40 Merc with the chopped top is the first of the dwarves to have AC and power rear windows.

All the wee rides contain standard features like working wipers, radio, heater, and defroster. The glove box opens, and wing windows swing out. Remember wings? The cars are registered with the DMV and cruise at highway speeds. Adams has been pulled over by the police, but it is always because officers want a closer look at the stylish ride.

Adams invests about 3,000 hours of labor in building each Dwarf car over 2 to 5 years. He and his tiny fleet have been featured on *Jay Leno's Garage* and *My Classic Car with Dennis Gage*. www.dwarfcarmuseum.com.

159. The biggest rattlesnake in the world startles traffic in Tucson.

And you can walk or ride a bicycle right through it. Rattlesnake Bridge stretches over Broadway Boulevard, 280 feet from its open mouth to its rattle-tipped tail. Tucson is known for its public art, and the big pedestrian bridge east of downtown is a classic example. Designed by artist Simon Donovan, the structure has won numerous awards for its innovative design. Iron beams double as shiny fangs. Structural posts represent the snake's ribs. The mesh covering is painted in repeating diamond patterns that perfectly match the reptiles slithering around in the desert. If motorists glance up as they drive underneath, they'll see lifelike scales carved in the concrete. The 20-foot-high tail is topped with a 300-pound fiberglass rattle that emits a sinister buzz as you walk past.

160. She's gonna blow! Arizona still has active volcanic fields.

Some of Arizona's most spectacular landscapes were born of violence. Volcanic activity lashed this corner of the world with a fire and a fury down through the ages that shaped much of the beauty we admire today.

There are seven young volcanic fields—young by geologic standards—in Arizona. The San Francisco Peaks, crowned by Humphreys Peak, are part of a hulking stratovolcano that once rose to 16,000 feet before blasting itself apart. The Colorado River in the Grand Canyon was damned several times by lava flow. The Superstition and Galiuro Mountains are composed largely of volcanic rock. The Chiricahua National

Sunset Crater, Arizona's youngest volcano erupting less than 1,000 years ago, is part of the San Francisco volcanic field. Courtesy of Mike Koopsen, Sedona.

Monument exists because the smothering crust of hardened volcanic ash eroded into a wonderland of spires, pinnacles, and hoodoos. Everywhere calderas, vents, cinder cones, lava tubes, and volcanic necks add character to the Arizona landscape.

Three of the volcanic fields are still active. Dormant but not extinct. The expansive San Francisco field covers 1,800 square miles near Flagstaff and is the site of the most recent eruption. Sunset Crater blew its top about 950 years ago. The Uinkaret volcanic field that sits on the North Rim of the Grand Canyon also broke bad magma-wise about 1,000 years ago.

And don't think for a minute it can't happen again. Although it's unlikely you'll need to cancel any travel plans. Eruptions have been reoccurring every few thousand years, and with hot spots still simmering deep beneath the earth's surface, scientists seem certain it will once again rain lava over northern Arizona sometime in the future.

161. Arizona has some of the thickest salt deposits in the world.

It isn't just copper, silver, and gold being dug from Arizona's rugged terrain. Massive deposits of rock salt are buried across the state, some that are thicker than the Grand Canyon is deep. The Luke Salt Body in Glendale covers 40 square miles and is more than a mile thick. Morton Salt has been mining it since the mid-1980s. They ship millions of bags of water-softening salt. One of the salt deposits near Kingman may be up to 10,000 feet thick or more. The Salt River is named for the salt deposits it flows past that were harvested by Native peoples for curing meats and medicinal purposes.

162. Butterflies love Arizona.

There are over 250 species of butterflies in the Sonoran Desert alone. And we get plenty of visitors migrating through. Only Texas has more butterfly species. And with people planting milkweed, we're seeing more and more monarchs wobbling through each year. The official state butterfly of Arizona is the two-tailed swallowtail, a beautiful creature with yellow wings fringed in black and nearly as big as a catcher's mitt.

A tiger swallowtail perches on a wild iris. Courtesy of Mike Koopsen, Sedona.

163. The town of Show Low is named for a card game.

In 1870 Marion Clark and Corydon Cooley were homesteading 100,000 acres in the White Mountains. But a few years later, the men had a falling out and decided to dissolve the partnership with a card game. They played a game called "Seven Up" long into the night. A weary Clark finally told Cooley, "Show low and you take the ranch." Cooley turned over the two of clubs. "Show low it is," he said, winning the land and providing the name of the future town. The main drag through Show Low is named Deuce of Clubs.

164. The town name of Snowflake has nothing to do with precipitation.

Snowflake is a picturesque town on the northern edge of the White Mountains. While it experiences all four seasons, it is not named for wintry weather. The town was founded in 1878 by Mormon pioneers and colonizers Erastus Snow and William Jordan Flake.

165. Despite sitting amid a massive pine forest, the town of Pinetop is not named for the trees.

Maybe. This is one of those tales that's hard to pin down as truth or legend. But it's a great legend, and keeps the theme of weird White Mountain town names going, so it's worth a mention. It all comes down to a saloonkeeper named Walt Rigney.

In the late 1880s, Johnny Phipps opened a store and saloon in a mountain meadow that became a popular watering hole for soldiers stationed at Fort Apache. After Phipps died, Rigney took over the establishment. Because he had a high unruly thatch of red hair, soldiers took to calling him "Pinetop." So when soldiers developed a thirst they would say, "Let's go to the top of the pines to see old Pinetop."

The town literally could not be named anything else.

166. There's only one cowboy college in the world, and where else could it be but in this Western land?

Arizona Cowboy College in Scottsdale teaches everything you need to know to ride the range. Wannabe punchers can saddle up for 1-, 2-, and 5-day sessions and learn the finer points of riding, roping, and working cattle. Even if you don't want to hire on with a ranch, or plan to take a herd over the trail, it's a nice way to spend a few days reconnecting with Arizona's deep-rooted cowboy history. (480) 471-3151, www.cowboycollege.com.

167. You'll find Nothing in Arizona.

Nothing sits in high desert along US 93 between Wickenburg and Wikieup. It once had a population of four and a couple of businesses. You could get gas or a cold drink on this lonely stretch of road. And sometimes that was enough. I remember standing in Nothing swilling a cold Coke and watching the setting sun paint the desert in soft golden hues. At that moment, Nothing was exactly where I wanted to be. Sadly, Nothing is a mere husk of that once-booming metropolis—just another ghost town being gnawed by the elements. But the sign remains, so you can always stop at Nothing in Arizona.

Almost nothing is left of Nothing—just a battered sign, crumbling buildings, and a lot of road-trip memories. Photo by the author.

My hope is that someone will move back and reopen Nothing. Because those little pauses add spice to any road trip. We should all be willing to stop at Nothing once in a while.

Some other town names seem just as odd. Arizona has towns named Why, Carefree, Surprise, Top-of-the-World, Bumble Bee, Skull Valley, Chloride, Tombstone, Bagdad, and Tuba City.

168. The curviest, loneliest federal highway in the country slithers down the mountains of eastern Arizona.

For years the Coronado Trail National Scenic Byway was known as the Devil's Highway. But if Lucifer was prone to carsickness, you can bet he wanted nothing to do with it.

The Coronado Trail, a segment of US 191, twists and turns for 123 miles between Morenci and Springerville in eastern Arizona. The road roughly parallels the New Mexico border, and it has the reputation of being the curviest and least-traveled federal highway in the country. Expect a 6,000-foot elevation change as it climbs from cactus-strewn desert to lush alpine meadows and aspen-clad mountains.

In Arizona the former US 666 was changed to the less demonic 191. Yet the road retains its beautiful but slightly sinister personality. It probably has something to do with the 460 curves, frightening drop-offs, and haunting quiet along the way. Francisco Vasquez de Coronado followed this route over 450 years ago as he searched for the Seven Cities of Gold, spawning the current name.

The road passes the mining towns of Clifton and Morenci and curves around one of the world's largest open-pit mines. It snakes its way up narrow Chase Canyon and switchbacks through scrubby woodland that gives way to dense pine forests as you climb. The Coronado Trail skirts the edge of the Blue Range Primitive Area, where Mexican gray wolves are released back into the wild.

Stop at the high perch of Blue Vista Point for the incredible views. Stop again at Hannagan Meadow Lodge for lunch and to breathe the cool mountain air. Oxygen at 9,100 feet just seems to have a fragrance all its own. Beyond Hannagan Meadow, the road softens its tone. The curves are lazier as it winds through forest still bearing the scars of 2012's Wallow Fire to Alpine, a lovely town ringed by mountains. From here, continue past brush-covered plateaus and the shimmering waters of Nelson Reservoir to the towns of Springerville and Eagar nestled in the Round Valley.

169. You'll find the world's largest skydiving center in Arizona.

Next time you're midway between Phoenix and Tucson, look up. You'll likely spot a bunch of people stepping out of airplanes at 13,000 feet above the desert floor. Located in Eloy, Skydive Arizona averages 135,000 jumps per year. It's the largest skydiving center in the world.

Attracted by the facilities and ideal weather conditions, skydivers come from all over for training camps and record-setting attempts. Skydive Arizona provides a huge drop zone surrounded by flat uninhabited desert. Their fleet is led by five Super Otters and seven Skyvans, each capable of taking up 23 skydivers. Along with a DC-3, they can put more than 240 skydivers in the air at any one time.

Another big attraction on the ground is SkyVenture Arizona, their large vertical wind chamber, 14 feet in diameter with wind speeds up to 150 miles per hour. Visitors can experience free fall without a parachute or jumping out of an airplane. (520) 466-3753, www.skydiveaz.com.

170. You can walk the entire length of the state.

The Arizona National Scenic Trail traverses the entire state south to north, stretching for over 800 miles. A Flagstaff teacher, Dale Shewalter, hatched the idea for the ambitious trail in the 1970s. It was a massive undertaking that involved cooperation from numerous state and federal agencies, along with an army of volunteers. Existing trails were knitted together with primitive roads and newer links. The long lanky path displays the rich and ever-changing scenery of Arizona, and was named a National Scenic Trail in 2009. Only 11 trails have received the prestigious designation. The Arizona Trail is divided into 43 passages. While many segments ramble through rugged backcountry, other portions are close to towns or are easily accessed making for good day-hiking possibilities all up and down the state, from top to bottom. www.aztrail.org.

171. Arizona has the absolute coolest Dairy Queen.

Sitting in the shadow of sandstone cliffs, in the heart of spectacular Oak Creek Canyon, travelers will find an old-school DQ. A skinny cousin of the Grand Canyon, Oak Creek Canyon is a gorge carved from the edge of the Mogollon Rim. It connects the red rock country of Sedona to the ponderosa pine forests of Flagstaff. Towering rock walls rise above lush woodlands. State Highway 89A traces the twists and turns of the clear running stream that carved the canyon. This was designated as the first scenic road in Arizona and is often named as one of the most beautiful in the nation. Dairy Queen sits about 4.5 miles north of Sedona with a full menu of food and ice cream goodies. As an added bonus, booths are set

(*Opposite page*) With its ever-changing scenery, the 800-mile long Arizona Trail attracts through-hikers, backpackers, and day hikers. Courtesy of Mike Koopsen, Sedona.

up in the Dairy Queen parking lot every day so Native American artists can display and sell their work. Make a spectacular red rock drive, stop to admire the views from Midgely Bridge, take a swim at Grasshopper Point if you get the urge, browse for bargains of beautiful Native artwork, then go inside for a Blizzard. Now that's an ice cream run you won't soon forget.

172. Sedona made McDonald's dance to their tasteful tune.

McDonald's may be a staggering behemoth in the world of fast food, but when they wanted to open one of their little burger bistros in red rock country, Sedona said, "Keep walking, clown town." They only agreed to let the project move forward if Mickey D's would abandon their trademark golden arches so as not to clash with the breath-stealing surroundings. That's why the Sedona McDonald's sports small, understated turquoise arches. It's the only McDonald's in the whole world adorned with that particular stylish hue.

173. We believe in truth in advertising.

A big town sign greets visitors to Gila Bend, the kind you're likely to find near the entrance to any small town. Almost. Look closer. The hand-painted sign says, "Gila Bend Welcomes You." It provides the current population and states that it is home to this many "friendly people," and also "5 old crabs." And just so you know they're not bluffing, a smaller sign below actually names the crabs!

It is my fervent hope that one day my hometown will adopt a similar sign, and I will be listed as one of the crabs. We all have dreams.

The only McDonald's in the world sporting turquoise arches can be found in Sedona. Courtesy of Mike Koopsen, Sedona.

Gila Bend wisely honors its most curmudgeonly citizens. Photo by the author.

174. The only four-story building in the country where every floor has a ground-level entrance was filled with Arizona kids.

Nothing highlights the slanted, sloping, mountainous terrain of Bisbee like the town's first high school, which was built in 1914. Set against a steep hill, the big structure included offices, classrooms, science labs, an ornate study hall, library, and a gymnasium on the highest floor. It stood four stories tall, and students could walk into each one from ground level. Such an architectural configuration resulted in the school being featured on *Ripley's Believe It or Not!* and in the Guinness Book of World Records.

As the mining industry boomed during the 1950s, the school could no longer contain the burgeoning student body. A new high school was built in 1959. Today the old building is used for Cochise County offices.

175. You can visit a mine that's like being trapped inside a rainbow.

The Hull Mine runs deep beneath the stark Castle Dome Mountains, north of Yuma. It's one of 300 mines gouged from the earth in this lonely corner of Arizona. The old silver mine dates back to the 1880s and was purchased in 2014 by Allen and Stephanie Armstrong, owners of the adjacent Castle Dome Mine Museum.

Their original plan for the Hull was to do what they did at Castle Dome, preserve a slice of Arizona history by restoring old buildings and salvaging equipment and materials. Everything changed once they got a look at the vibrant wonders inside the mine. That's when they set up the tours.

Visitors are driven down the main passageway to a wide corridor,

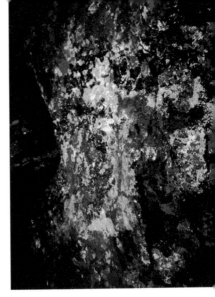

The walls of the Hull Mine blaze with color when illuminated with UV lighting. Photo by the author.

100 vertical feet below the surface. From there it's a short stroll to the end of one drift. At first the high walls look no different than any others towering overhead. But when the lights are clicked off and UV lights hum to life, it's only seconds before the rocks begin to bleed color.

Out of the darkness leaps a Jackson Pollock design. A spray of vivid hues is streaked across the walls, forming a wild abstract display. Blues, reds, yellows, oranges, greens, and some colors that have not yet been named are spread up and down.

While it may seem like magic, it's simply the result of fluorescent and phosphorescent minerals. These are minerals that emit visible light when exposed to ultraviolet radiation. If the mineral continues to glow after the light has been removed, this is called phosphorescence. The minerals setting the walls ablaze at the Hull are calcite, fluorite, scheelite, willemite, barite, hydrozincite, aragonite, and selenite.

The Hull Mine is like the juicy parts of a kaleidoscope. These are fossilized fireworks, the neon of caveman times. This is a snow globe filled not with the white stuff but with the northern lights. This is the graffiti of ghosts.

After leaving the dazzling color show behind, there's still the rest of the mine to tour. Walk back down the level passageway to where an exposed vein of silver galena streaks the ceiling. Other corridors are filled with artifacts left behind, like tools, goods, and blacksmith equipment. Another drift leads to a desperado's hideaway. Instead of fleeing the area after a shootout or robbery, local badmen commonly hid out in abandoned mine shafts.

Castle Dome Mine Museum features more than 50 buildings, filled to the rafters with artifacts. There's a restored stamp mill, cemetery, and a self-guided hiking trail, all in the shadow of rugged mountains. This is Arizona's most comprehensive exploration of daily life in a frontier mining town. (928) 920-3062, www.enchantedcavern.org.

176. Arizona is one of the largest producers of the world's oldest cultivated fruit.

Dates have been cultivated in the Middle East for at least 6,000 years. The fruit was prized as a source of nutrition wrapped in a sugary sweet, easily transported package. With their rich succulence and natural sweetness, medjool dates were the most cherished of all. These plump soft dates were once reserved for Moroccan royalty.

Medjools arrived in the United States in 1927 as part of a rescue mission. When disease ravaged the medjool crop in Morocco, an American horticulturist took 11 medjool shoots to California, forming the foundation of that crop. Then they made their way to Yuma with its date-friendly climate—lots of hot sunshine and an abundance of groundwater.

Today, medjools are considered a superfood, low in fat but high in fiber, potassium, antioxidants, and loaded with vitamins. Their natural sugars make them especially desirable. It's like growing candy on trees. But a very labor-intensive candy that requires workers to climb the tall trees multiple times during the season. Medjools are the primary date

Workers climb each of Yuma's date palm trees multiple times throughout the growing season as they prepare to harvest the fruit. Photo by the author.

consumed in the United States, and Yuma is a major producer of the luscious fruit.

Bonus fact: date shakes are heavenly!

177. The beloved Black Sphinx date grows only in a single Phoenix neighborhood.

I'm fudging this fact a little, but it was true for decades.

A curious-looking date palm seedling was discovered in Phoenix in 1928 and replanted. It was believed to be descended from an ancient date variety, the hayani. That original mother plant went on to be the source for hundreds of trees, which made up the original grove of Black Sphinx date palms in Arcadia, east of Phoenix.

The tall regal trees produce a remarkable date. The small plump dark-skinned fruit has a creamy texture and a honey flavor with notes of vanilla and caramel. Black Sphinx dates are more delicate than medjools and harder to transport long distances. So they've mostly remained a regional delicacy.

As Phoenix continued to grow, the date ranch was sold and divided into housing plots, becoming the Mountgrove neighborhood. Many homeowners still harvest and sell their own Black Sphinx dates. The dates remain extremely rare. The original trees still left are reaching the end of their fruit-producing days. A few trees have been started from offshoots in other small groves around Phoenix, and some traveled to Yuma. Since they have a short shelf life and a limited harvest, word spreads quickly among aficionados when the Black Sphinx is available in the early fall. Look for them at the Sphinx Date Co. Palm & Pantry. 3039 N. Scottsdale Rd., (480) 941-2261, www.sphinxdateranch.com.

178. We're the only state that has a national park and a national monument dedicated to the preservation of cactus.

Two sections of Saguaro National Park bookend the city of Tucson. Here you'll find virtual forests of our iconic saguaros marching up mountain slopes. The spiny giants create the perfect foreground for Tucson's signature sky-fire sunsets. Both the east-side Rincon Mountain District and the Tucson Mountain District at the western edge of town feature scenic drives and multiple hiking trails. (520) 733-5153, www.nps.gov/sagu.

Organ Pipe Cactus National Monument perches on the Mexican border south of Ajo, and preserves over 500 square miles of pristine desert. All told, 31 species of cactus can be found in the park, including the namesake

Organ Pipe Cactus National Monument is a biosphere reserve protecting its namesake and dozens of other cactus species. Photo by the author.

organ pipe. Unlike the saguaro that rises in a single trunk, the organ pipe is a furious clutter of segments shooting up from the base. The monument is one of the few spots where the large cactus grows north of Mexico.

In 1976, the United Nations recognized the diversity of the monument by naming it an International Biosphere Reserve. The designation has attracted scientists from around the world, who conduct studies on this intact Sonoran Desert ecosystem. (520) 387-6849, www.nps.gov/orpi.

179. Arizona has the world's first international electric vehicle museum.

Electric vehicles seem hip and trendy these days, but there is nothing new about them. In fact, electric cars have been around since the 1830s. Opened in 2014, the Route 66 Electric Vehicle Museum in Kingman displays a wide range of conveyances that include electric micro-cars dating back to the 1940s, the world's first electric street rod, and the extremely rare 1909 Elwell-Parker baggage tug—one of only two known to exist. The collection was first housed, appropriately enough, in the Powerhouse. The hulking concrete building provided electricity to the region at the beginning of the 20th century. (As their collection of electric vehicles continues to grow, the museum may expand to a larger space downtown.) Today, the Powerhouse Visitor Center provides information to Kingman visitors and Route 66 travelers. (928) 753-6106, www.explorekingman.com.

180. There's a masterpiece painted across the boulders of a lonely canyon.

Imagine if Leonardo da Vinci put the Mona Lisa not on canvas but on a rock. Or a bunch of rocks, and then left them to bake in the Arizona sun. That's what artist Roy Purcell did in 1966 when he painted a set of murals called *The Journey* on towering slabs of granite in a canyon just outside of the tiny town of Chloride.

Purcell was an art student who worked part time as a miner when he created the 2,000-square-foot murals. He returned 40 years later to repaint the vivid scenes that include a writhing serpent, a rising goddess, ancient symbols, and a community threatened by a giant bird foot with talons. Like all good art, the murals slap you around a little. They can be viewed by traveling just over a mile on a dirt road. Look for ancient rock art adorning surrounding boulders in this open-air exhibit.

The Journey launched Purcell's professional career. Chloride, nestled at the base of the Cerbat Mountains north of Kingman, is considered Arizona's oldest

Colorful murals painted by Roy Purcell spread across a large boulder field outside of the mining town of Chloride. Photo by the author.

continuously occupied mining town. A handful of shops are open for business, and there's usually a restaurant or two serving grub. Pay attention as you wander the tiny town because almost every home sports some weird quirky folk art.

181. The world's highest concrete arch bridge stretches from Arizona into Nevada.

The Mike O'Callaghan–Pat Tillman Memorial Bridge measures 1,900 feet long and soars 890 feet above the Colorado River. Construction was completed in 2010 to bypass the twisting crowded drive across Hoover Dam. Pedestrian access to the bridge is provided for tourists who want to enjoy broad panoramas of the dam and river below. It incorporates the widest concrete arch in the Western Hemisphere and is the second-highest bridge in the United States, after the Royal Gorge Bridge in Colorado. It is the world's highest concrete arch span.

Mike O'Callaghan was a decorated Korean War veteran and governor of Nevada during the 1970s. Pat Tillman had been a star football player for the Arizona State University and the Arizona Cardinals. Following the 9/11 attack he gave up his professional football career to enlist in the US Army. He was killed by friendly fire in Afghanistan in 2004.

182. A unique Arizona memorial spotlights veterans for one minute each year.

The Anthem Veterans Memorial is an elegant tribute all year round, but it truly comes to life for a single minute. Five pillars, staggered in size, are perfectly aligned with elliptical openings. At exactly 11:11 a.m. on Veteran's Day (November 11), the sun streams through, shining a solar spotlight on a mosaic of the Great Seal of the United States positioned in front of them.

The pillars represent the unity of the United States military serving steadfast together. Each bears an insignia with the order of the branches placed in accordance with Department of Defense protocol—Army, Marine Corps, Navy, Air Force, and Coast Guard. A Circle of Honor surrounds the monument and contains hundreds of paving stones engraved with the names of veterans. The red pavers, white pillars, and blue Arizona sky represent Old Glory.

It was quite an impressive feat for engineers to capture the precise angle of the sun to illuminate the seal at the exact right minute. Even with yearly variations, the monument will remain accurate within a 12-second range for hundreds of years. Located at 41703 N. Gavilan Peak Parkway in Anthem, the monument is copyrighted so it cannot be reproduced anywhere else.

183. The world's largest museum of firefighting history remains an undiscovered gem in Phoenix.

What started as a private collection of restored fire engines has evolved into the Hall of Flame Museum of Firefighting. An acre in size, the Hall of Flame spreads across six exhibit galleries and includes more than 120 wheeled vehicles, plus steamers, hand pumpers, international equipment, and thousands of smaller artifacts, the oldest dating back to 1725. A couple of poignant exhibits include Rescue 4, a fire truck from New York City that responded to the call on 9/11 and sustained considerable damage when the Twin Towers fell. Tragically, all eight crewmembers of Rescue 4 perished. Museum volunteers worked diligently for 2 years to restore Rescue 4, and now it serves as a lovely tribute to the crew and all who were lost that day.

Closer to home, the Hall of Flame also includes one of the transport trucks for the Granite Mountain Hotshots, the 19 firefighters who died while battling Arizona's Yarnell Hill Fire in 2013. But don't think for a moment this is a solemn place. It's full of life and color and laughter. Classrooms of elementary-school kids are always passing through on field trips for tours and fire safety classes and to scramble around on a big bright fire truck parked in the children's play area for just that purpose. Every room is filled with wildland equipment, air tanks, horse-drawn trucks, parade vehicles, patches, models, and more. Most of the staff and volunteers are retired firefighters, so you can thank them personally for their service. 6101 E. Van Buren St., (602) 275-3473, www.hallofflame.org.

184. An Arizona road inspired a hit song.

While touring the Southwest in the early 1970s, Gordon Lightfoot spotted a poetic road sign. Driving north from Phoenix, the Canadian singer and songwriter passed the Carefree Highway as it rambled across open desert bristling with tall saguaros. The Carefree Highway runs east from Interstate 17 to the town of Carefree, and travels west from the interstate toward Wickenburg as State Highway 74.

Lightfoot jotted down the name and a few months later penned one of his biggest hits. "Carefree Highway" came out in 1974 and reached No. 1 on Billboard's easy listening charts and No. 10 on the Billboard Hot 100. It's a sweet, wistful tune about a man reminiscing over a long-lost love. And it conjures up something in all of us. At one time or another, everyone yearns for his or her own carefree highway, a simple escape from trials and troubles. If you can just jump in your car and go far enough, nothing else seems to matter.

"Carefree Highway, let me slip away, slip away on you."

185. A desert waterhole led to world-famous pies.

A natural spring in the desert is a pretty big deal. Having a steady source of water made this a stagecoach stop just north of Phoenix. In 1918, enterprising Ben Warner erected a canvas-covered store while he worked on additional buildings in the area known as Rock Springs.

Warner hauled gasoline in 5-gallon cans to sell, and the water was always needed to fill radiators for motorists about to climb the steep mountains on their way to Prescott. By 1924 a hotel, general store, and restaurant were open. Apparently, Warner also ran a still during Prohibition, selling a little moonshine on the sly. Rock Springs Café was a watering hole in every sense.

It was Mrs. Warner who began making pies for the restaurant—pies that would become a signature item. Today, gasoline is dispensed from pumps. The hotel rooms where screen legends Jean Harlow and Tom Mix once slept are shuttered. And mason jars of home-brewed hooch are no longer available. But pies have become synonymous with the name Rock Springs.

More than 100,000 pies are sold each year at Rock Springs Café. In keeping with the times, they now ship all over the country with more than two dozen to choose from, including beauties like cherry crumb, chocolate cream, Tennessee lemon,

Travelers used to stop at Rock Springs Café for water and moonshine, but these days it's all about the pies. Courtesy of Rick Mortensen, Cincinnati.

and lattice-top apple. But their number-one seller—and a personal weakness of mine—is the Jack Daniel's pecan pie.

The long history of alcohol at Rock Springs pays off with this wheel of gooey goodness. Topped by the soft crunch of Arizona-grown pecans, this pie is impossibly light and luscious with a lingering note of caramel. When water is found in the desert, all sorts of wonderful things can happen. (623) 374-5794, www.rocksprings.cafe.

186. We have a sky-spearing fountain with a whole town built around it.

Fountain Hills was established in 1970 as a master planned community. Robert McCulloch built the centerpiece fountain that same year, just months before the reconstruction of a little trinket he picked up in England known as London Bridge.

Driven by three 600 horsepower turbine pumps, the fountain blasts 7,000 gallons of water through an 18-inch nozzle. With all three pumps running, the spray reaches 560 feet in height. It held the title as the world's tallest fountain for more than a decade.

Since then other taller fountains have gushed forth, some using rivers and others set in the ocean, which seems to be an unfair advantage. So now Fountain Hills has reduced their claim to the "World's Tallest Continuously Running Freshwater Fountain." Maybe it is a little hairsplitty but still impressive for the middle of the desert.

One of the world's tallest fountains still shows off its stuff at the top of each hour, launching a geyser of water for 15 minutes. Usually only two pumps are running, shooting the water to a height of 300 or so feet. And the pumps won't operate on windy days to keep folks enjoying a lakeside walk from getting soaked. On special occasions, the town still lets the fountain cut loose full force, and that's quite a spectacle.

Fountain Hills is home to more than 100 publicly displayed pieces of artwork. The eight fountains along the Avenue of Fountains kicked off the community's public art collection. (480) 816-5185, www.experience fountainhills.org.

187. Castles dot the Phoenix landscape.

If they decide to film a *Downton Abbey* prequel in Arizona, we've got the necessary ingredients. Plus, unlike those bland European castles, ours actually come with a little history.

There is a distinctive bit of melancholy attached to Mystery Castle. Rising in the foothills of South Mountain Park, Mystery Castle was built in the 1930s by Boyce Luther Gulley for his daughter Mary Lou Gulley. Yet she wouldn't see it until after his death. After learning he had tuberculosis, Gulley moved from Seattle to Phoenix and began building the sprawling castle using traditional materials as well as found objects like recycled car parts, telephone poles, and plow discs. The 18 rooms in the 3-story castle include a chapel, cantina, and dungeon. When Gulley died in 1945, Mary Lou and her mother were notified they had inherited the property. They moved in and soon afterward began offering tours. Mary Lou lived in Mystery Castle until her death in 2010. The property is now maintained by a foundation, and tours are still offered. www.mymystery castle.com.

Bearing a striking resemblance to a wedding cake, Tovrea Castle was built by an Italian immigrant named Alessio Carraro. His vision to create a hotel and desert resort surrounded by a cactus garden never panned out, and the pinewood and stucco building was sold off to E. A. and Della Tovrea in 1931. It was later purchased by the City of Phoenix, and both the building and gardens were restored. Now known as Tovrea

Although Tovrea Castle never became the desert resort envisioned by its builder, the distinctive structure makes a fine Phoenix park. Photo by the author.

Castle at Carraro Heights, honoring the previous owners and the original builder, it is part of the Phoenix parks system. Tours are offered during cooler months. (602) 256-3221, www.tovreacastletours.com.

188. The tequila sunrise was invented at the Arizona Biltmore.

A bartender named Gene Sulit created the cocktail a long time ago. But it was different than the contemporary version.

Built in 1929 the Arizona Biltmore was a posh playground for Hollywood stars like Clark Gable and Frank Sinatra. The swimming pool at the

Frank Lloyd Wright–inspired resort was rumored to be Marilyn Monroe's favorite. And Irving Berlin penned several songs while relaxing poolside. (One Arizona legend claims Berlin wrote "White Christmas" at the Biltmore, but that does not appear to be true. Great story, though.)

Sometime in the 1930s a guest requested a refreshing tequila drink to cut through the Arizona heat. Sulit went to work. He poured the tequila, along with black currant liqueur, crème de cassis. He added lime juice, soda water, and ice. A new cocktail was born, the Biltmore tequila sunrise. While the tequila sunrise underwent a transformation many years later, with orange juice and grenadine now being key ingredients, you can still order the classic version at the Biltmore, which retains its Gatsby-esque charm. Have it as you lie by the pool on a warm sunny day in December while humming "White Christmas" and ogling the ghost of Marilyn Monroe. Hey, I think I just decided how I want to spend the holidays. www.arizonabiltmore.com.

189. America's largest town is in Arizona.

Gilbert sits southeast of Phoenix. The rural community was known as the "Hay Capital of the World" during World War I and into the 1920s because local farmers supplied so much hay for US Army horses. A more modern version of Gilbert began to take shape in the 1970s when the town council annexed 53 square miles of land. It wasn't long before growth exploded.

Today, a quarter of a million people reside in Gilbert, known for its vibrant dining scene, eclectic shops, art galleries, and walkable downtown. It often shows up on national lists for "Most Livable Cities," "Best Cities to Raise a Family," "Safest Cities," that sort of thing. But here's what's not quite accurate about those articles: Gilbert is not a city, but a town. It is the largest town in the country.

In Arizona, cities and towns have the same rights, yet there is still a legal distinction. Only a city can elect council members to represent defined districts. A town holds "at large" elections, meaning all elected officials serve the town as a whole. A city can draw up a charter, but a town cannot. To become a city requires Gilbert to take legal steps toward that designation, and, despite their growing population, they have so far declined to do so.

In this case, the numbers don't tell the whole story. While the growth is undeniable, the small-town spirit remains. The Gilbert water tower is still a seminal piece of architecture anchoring downtown, which has been converted into the Heritage District featuring an enticing blend of local restaurants and shops, a theater, museum, and several little pocket parks and other outdoor spaces. Best of all, every business seems to be adorned with an old-school neon sign adding a cascade of light and color to every evening stroll. Festivals and events are regular occurrences because Gilbert grabs any excuse to throw a shindig. There's something hip yet sweetly old-timey about it.

The word *town* conjures up a slower pace in a family-friendly community where smiles are common. In Gilbert people know their neighbors—and even if they don't, they are still willing to treat folks neighborly. Now that's one big town. (480) 503-6000, www.discover gilbert.com.

190. Our neon burns brightly.

Downtown Gilbert is not the only place where neon saturates the night sky. Arizona has a long history with neon. A bristling forest of colorful signs blaze the way along cross-country highways like Route 66, called America's Main Street, and Route 80, known as the Broadway of America.

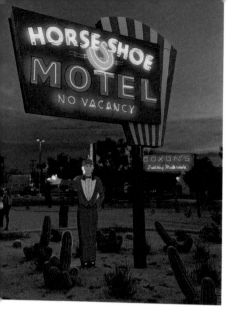

Visitors to Casa Grande Neon Sign Park are transported to a different era. Photo by the author.

A healthy population of the old signs remain, some still in original condition, some restored. New ones are added to the mix each year. Williams on Route 66 is a shimmering, glimmering hotbed of neon. Drive through town at night and enjoy a velvet constellation of color. In Tucson, a 30-foot-tall neon saguaro welcomes visitors from the median of Oracle Road (once Highway 80). Another dozen beautifully restored vintage signs act as beacons on the road.

Neon connects us to the road trips of our youth. Before Yelp and Tripadvisor, it was neon that told us where to eat and sleep. Instead of squinting at our phones for guidance, we simply peered out the windshield at lights that moved and danced, and made our choices. Carving the night into rainbow hues, neon felt like equal parts chemistry and magic. Neon is the nightlight of angels and drunkards.

A surprising treasure trove of neon can be found in the small desert community of Casa Grande. In 2019, the town opened the cozy Neon Sign Park at the edge of downtown. Now every evening at dusk, they flip the switch and flood the night with a medley of hues. The park features 14 signs of mostly local origin that have been salvaged and rehabilitated. Rustic benches made from old truck tailgates are positioned amid landscaped walking paths throughout the small park.

The neon is personal here. The signs are removed from their once-lofty perches and positioned not for traffic but for pedestrians. They hang just overhead, a treetop nebula. The glow is warm as summer moonlight. Colors are as juicy as fresh-picked fruit. In the deepening dusk a graceful cascade of fireworks drop from above and remind visitors of more innocent times. www.neonsignpark.com.

191. The only Native American owned and operated zoo in the United States is here.

Known as "a Sanctuary for Nature and the Spirit," the Navajo Nation Zoo provides shelter for rescued animals. More than 50 animal species native to tribal lands are here. Nearly all the animals came to the zoo because they were injured or orphaned in the wild. Informational signage teaches more than just standard biology. Visitors also learn the traditional Navajo stories relating to the animals.

Located in Window Rock, the Navajo Nation capital, this is the only Native American zoo in the country. One of the zoo's goals is to help the Navajo people maintain their link to the natural world through native plants and animals. The spacious Eagle Sanctuary contains non-releasable golden eagles and serves as a legal source of molted feathers for Navajos and other Native Americans. 34 Highway 264, (928) 871-6574, www.navajozoo.org.

192. Arizona diners eat pizza while being entertained by the lush tones of the world's largest Wurlitzer pipe organ.

This cavernous place is not your typical neighborhood pizza parlor. Organ Stop Pizza is the size of a warehouse with ceilings 43 feet high,

Every pizza becomes an event when it's accompanied by the lush tones of the giant Wurlitzer at Organ Stop Pizza in Mesa. Photo by the author.

spread between two levels with long communal tables and seating for 700. Then the music starts, rich and luscious, surrounding you, filling every corner of the big hall, and the place suddenly feels as intimate as a corner bistro.

Organ Stop Pizza has been a beloved destination in Mesa since 1975. The building it now occupies was designed specifically to house the massive Wurlitzer theater organ and to achieve optimum acoustics. More than 6,000 pipes form the back wall of the restaurant. Many of the percussions like xylophones, cymbals, glockenspiels, and drums are installed in the dining room. It feels like patrons are seated inside the giant organ.

The organist commands everyone's attention from his position front and center at the elevated console with 1,050 individual keys, buttons, and switches. Song selection ranges from classical to big band to Disney favorites. In addition, the organist operates the elaborate theatrical and lighting effects. It's a memorable show to go along with your pizza.

Organ Stop's mighty Wurlitzer was originally installed in 1927 in the Denver Theater. During the silent movie era, theater organs were played during the film to provide a live soundtrack. Once talkies began, the instruments fell out of favor. Organ Stop rebuilt and continued to expand their Wurlitzer until it has become the largest theater pipe organ of any type to be assembled. 1149 E. Southern Ave., Mesa, (480) 813-5700, www.organstoppizza.com.

193. Like the Egyptians, we entomb our leaders in pyramids.

At least we did once. The body of Arizona's first governor, George Wylie Paul Hunt, lies inside a pyramid atop a hill in Papago Park. A colorful character, Hunt was short and bald with a handlebar mustache, and weighed nearly 300 pounds.

Born in Missouri, Hunt traveled west at an early age and settled in Globe in 1881. He kicked around with odd jobs before entering public service. The self-made

Arizona's first, and oft re-elected, governor George W. P. Hunt is entombed in a pyramid atop a hill in Papago Park. Photo by the author.

man became the first mayor of Globe and later served in the Territorial Legislature. Hunt would go on to be one of the architects of the Arizona Constitution, serving as the state's first governor. He would be elected governor seven times but not always in order. Hunt was Arizona's first, second, third, sixth, seventh, eighth, and tenth governor. That's bound to be some kind of record.

After his death on Christmas Eve 1934, he was interred in the white pyramid amid the red buttes of Papago Park in Phoenix.

194. The world's only global musical instrument museum rocks out in Phoenix.

Most museums are quiet experiences with people speaking in hushed tones as they creep past exhibits. There's probably not a lot of toe tapping happening. But everybody gets their groove on at the Musical Instrument Museum (MIM). The sprawling facility showcases instruments and music of cultures from around the world and is a must visit for families. Displaying over 8,000 instruments collected from 200 countries and territories, this is the only musical instrument museum with such a global collection.

Permanent galleries are organized by geography and are complemented by lavish special exhibitions. Most displays are enhanced by state-of-the-art audio and video technologies that allow guests to see the instruments, hear their sounds, and observe them being played. As you move from one exhibit to the next, your wireless headset picks up the audio of the screen as you approach. Funky and futuristic. Guests even get to jam with a range of axes in the Experience Gallery. The MIM Music Theater hosts over 200 concerts a year. 4725 E. Mayo Blvd., (480) 478-6000, www.mim.org.

A few motivated citizens in Scottsdale organized to protect their beloved desert landscape by creating the expansive McDowell Sonoran Preserve. Photo by the author.

195. McDowell Sonoran Preserve is the largest city park in the United States.

The Scottsdale preserve sprawls across 30,500 contiguous acres with 225 miles of interconnected trails weaving through unspoiled desert. This feels like a place that shouldn't exist—prime real estate snatched away from developers. A few passionate activists hatched a plan to save a vast swath of desert terrain. They formed the McDowell Sonoran Conservancy and fought to protect the mountains and desert of North Scottsdale, most of which was private land ripe for development. The grassroots effort continued to expand despite overwhelming odds. Political leaders finally got on board, and Scottsdale residents voted not once but twice in favor of a sales tax increase to raise money to purchase the land. The result is the largest urban preserve (not counting state and federal parks) in the United States, a crown jewel of city planning and a reminder that just a few determined people can make a difference.

Established in 1994, the McDowell Sonoran Preserve is larger than the entire neighboring city of Tempe. Thanks to the concentrated efforts of the community, nearly one-third of Scottsdale remains pristine, public open space. Visitors to the preserve will discover a land of soaring mountains, boulder-crowned mesas, storm-carved arroyos, and dense cactus groves. (480) 998-7971, www.mcdowellsonoran.org.

If you're wondering what the second-largest urban park is, you just need to mosey over to Phoenix. At more than 16,000 acres, South Mountain Park is nearly 20 times larger than New York City's Central Park.

196. Every resident of Arizona lives within 15 minutes of a hiking trail.

OK, this is a fact I made up, but I'll bet it's true. For people in small towns like me, it's closer than that. But even for folks in the heart of Phoenix, trails are everywhere.

There is no other urban area like the Valley of the Sun in the United States. Millions of people, yet hundreds of miles of hiking trails, open desert, and rugged mountains, right on their doorsteps. That instant access to wild country is a rare quality-of-life issue. Drop me off at any house in Arizona, and I'm sure I can quickly find my way to a trail.

197. A Tucson nonprofit prepares to feed the world in case of drought, pestilence, or zombie apocalypse.

Native Seeds/SEARCH seeks to preserve crop diversity of the Southwest from the ground up. They maintain an extensive seed bank of nearly 2,000 varieties of crops adapted to these arid landscapes, many of which are rare or endangered. Working with conservation gardens and small

Hikers admire the well-earned view from atop Camelback Mountain, part of the extensive trail system found in the Phoenix metropolitan area. Photo by the author.

farmers, they regenerate a portion of the collection each year at different sites. They return some seeds to long-term cold storage and sell the surplus. Those proceeds enable them to distribute heirloom seeds for free to Native Americans, keeping agricultural traditions alive and maintaining a wide pool of genetic diversity to assure food security no matter what the future holds. (520) 622-0830, www.nativeseeds.org.

198. Arizona has one of the highest-elevation botanical gardens in the nation.

The Arboretum of Flagstaff is a botanical garden, nature center, and environmental education station sheltered in a ponderosa pine forest at an elevation of 7,150 feet. Despite the short growing season, more than 750 species of plants can be found among the dozen themed gardens such as forest meadow, pollinator garden, riparian habitat, and shade garden. Plants spill from beds and crowd the pathways, which attracts an abundance of birds and wildlife.

Spread across 200 acres, the arboretum makes a serene and very personal escape. Originally, it was the home of Frances McAllister. In 1981, she donated the land and created an endowment as part of her dream to preserve this magnificent swath of forest. The arboretum features multiple events throughout the season including a concert series, wildflower walks, and plant sales. 4001 S. Woody Mountain Rd., (928) 774-1442, www.thearb.org.

199. You can take a train to nowhere in Arizona and have a fantastic day.

At the Verde Canyon Railroad they like to remind everyone that it's not the destination, it's the journey that's important. Then they prove it. The train pulls out of the depot in Clarkdale and rolls through a riparian corridor carved by the Verde River. The water is canopied by cottonwoods as sunlight sparkles on the surface. High sandstone cliffs cradle the bottomlands under skies achingly blue. Such collision of ecosystems lures a variety of wildlife, notably eagle, hawk, heron, mule deer, javelina, coyote, and beaver. It's a fur and feather roster that makes Verde Canyon Railroad the envy of other adventure tours.

During the four-hour journey, the train travels along a section of standard-gauge track originally laid in 1911 to support the mining activity of Jerome, a roaring, wide-open boomtown that produced over a billion dollars in copper ore.

Narration is piped through the public address system, covering subjects like geology, archaeology, ornithology, and the history of the region. Vintage FP7 diesel locomotives provide the power for Verde Canyon Railroad. Passenger cars are refurbished for comfort and feature

Verde Canyon Railroad travels a historic train track into a remote and scenic corner of Arizona—and then returns. Photo by the author.

panoramic windows. Yet much of the ride will be spent aboard the open-air viewing cars that are impossible to resist.

The scenery pulls you outside. The route, inaccessible by other means, traces the river into rugged red-cliff canyon country akin to nearby Sedona. Along the way, the train rumbles across trestles and through a curved 680-foot tunnel. After 20 miles the train stops at the ghost ranch of Perkinsville, where scenes for the movie *How the West Was Won* were filmed. The engines are sidetracked, hooked to the other end of the train, and the return trip to Clarkdale begins.

Here's what makes the trip truly special: since the summer of 2020, I'm the official narrator for Verde Canyon Railroad. So not only do you get to ride to nowhere, you listen to me blab while you're going. How can you resist?

Verde Canyon Railroad offers different themed trains throughout the year including Saturday Night Starlight Rides, Fall Colors, Eagle Watch, and Ales on Rails. (800) 582-7245, www.verdecanyonrr.com.

200. Arizona has the nation's only tumbleweed Christmas tree.

And it's a beauty! This unique Chandler tradition dates back to 1957, when the first tumbleweed Christmas tree was unveiled. City workers begin rounding up tumbleweeds in October. The plants are Russian thistle bushes, an invasive species that break off from the roots at the end of their life to begin their wandering ways. Crews gather 1,000 of the rolling desert vagabonds to form the Christmas tree.

The tumbleweeds are piled onto a wire frame, squished and smashed into a plump cone shape. They're sprayed with gallons of flame retardant and gloss white paint. While the paint is still wet, crews bombard the creation with 80 pounds of glitter. It's then wrapped in holiday lights for a big festive package.

It all proves to be surprisingly lovely. Standing 35 feet tall and 20 feet wide, the tumbleweed tree is the centerpiece of Chandler's holiday season. The annual tree lighting draws thousands of spectators and includes a huge parade through downtown. So for once, the tumbleweeds get to stay still while people roll past.

Sometimes we just like to do things a little differently in Arizona.

Bonus Fact: Our sunsets are masterpieces of light and color.

If you believe this is opinion and not fact, you have not spent much time in Arizona.

Courtesy of Mike Koopsen, Sedona.

Courtesy of Mike Koopsen, Sedona.

Courtesy of Mike Koopsen, Sedona.

Awesome Arizona: 200 Amazing Facts about the Grand Canyon State

Topical Guide

(Numbers represent fact numbers in the book.)

EVENTS

Bisbee 1000 Craft Beer Festival, 73

Bisbee 1000 The Great Stair Climb, 73

Bisbee Coaster Race, 138

Cactus League, 86

Copper Classic, 87

Dillinger Days, 111

Field to Feast, 4

La Fiesta de los Vaqueros, 16

Hashknife Pony Express, 144

New Year's celebrations, 94

Parada del Sol, 144

Sidewalk Egg Fry, 36

Tombstone Rose Festival, 51

Tumbleweed Christmas Tree Lighting, 200

World's Oldest Continuous Rodeo, 16

World's Oldest Rodeo, 16

FOOD AND DRINK

Chimichanga, 147, 148

Dairy Queen, 171

Dates, 1, 176, 177

El Charro Café, 147, 148

Floating tiki bar, 77

James Beard Award, 149

McDonald's, 19, 172

Organ Stop Pizza, 192

Phantom Ranch Canteen, 145

Rock Springs Café, 185

Room 4 Bar, 76

Saloons, historic, 75

Sonoran hot dog, 149

Tequila, 74, 188

Tequila sunrise, 188

Tucson, UNESCO City of Gastronomy, 146

Winter vegetables, 4

GRAND CANYON

Airplane crash, 61

Astronaut training, 65

Colter, Mary, 137, 145

California condors, 128

Dark skies, 81

Grand Canyon rattlesnake, 84

Hiking, 29, 142, 145

Ives, Joseph Christmas, 140

Kolb brothers, 141

Life zones, 66

Mail delivery, 12

Mooney Falls/Cheyava Falls, 29

Natural wonder, 2, 142

Phantom Ranch, 12, 137, 142, 145

Rock squirrel, 139

Thunder River, 62

Volcanic activity, 160

GREAT OUTDOORS

Agassiz Peak, 24

Antelope Canyon, 60

Boyce Thompson Arboretum, 132

Chiricahua National Monument, 6, 81, 160

Deserts, other, 10, 34

Galiuro Mountains, 160

Gila Box Riparian National Conservation Area, 152

Grand Falls, 29

Horseshoe Bend, 79

Humphreys Peak, 24, 38, 66, 160

Lake Havasu, 30, 34, 35, 71, 77

Lake Mead, 95

Lake Powell, 60, 95

Mazatzal Mountains, 144

Meteor Crater, 11, 65

Mogollon Rim, 7, 17, 18, 48, 171

Mooney Falls, 29

Mountains, most, 9

Mount Graham, 26, 98, 101

National monuments, 6

Oak Creek Canyon, 171

Organ Pipe Cactus National Monument, 6, 178

Petrified Forest National Park, 6, 81, 89

Picacho Peak, 47

Pinaleño Mountains, 100, 101

Ponderosa pine forest, 7, 8, 17, 66, 67, 165, 171, 198

Saguaro National Park, 6, 178

San Pedro Riparian National Conservation Area, 42, 152

Sky Islands, 97, 100, 101, 128

Sonoran Desert, 6, 10, 14, 34, 46, 98, 129, 144, 153, 162, 178

Sunset Crater, 6, 65, 160

Superstition Mountains, 133, 160

Tonto Natural Bridge State Park, 22

Verde Canyon Railroad, 199

Vermilion Cliffs National Monument, 6, 68, 128, 143

Wave, the, 143

Wilderness areas, 68

HISTORY

Ancestral Puebloans, 27

Anza, Juan Bautista de, 153

Arizona counties, 26

Arizona Navy, 31

Arizona, 48th State, 43

Ashfork-Bainbridge Dam, 118

Aztec Land and Cattle Company, 144

Beale Wagon Road, 116

Billy the Kid, 49, 56

Canyon Diablo, 78

Casa Grande Ruins National Monument, 109

Civil War, 46, 47

Climax Jim, 23

Clovis culture, 42

Colter, Mary 137, 145

Dendrochronology, 67

Dillinger, John, 111

El Tiradito Wishing Shrine, 5

Federal Aviation Administration, 61

GPS development, 21

Hall, Sharlot Madbrith, 130

Hunt, George Wylie Paul, 193

Jails/prisons, 23, 78, 110, 112, 113, 114, 121

Kitt Peak National Observatory, 80

Kolb brothers, 141

Lehner Mammoth-Kill Site, 42

London Bridge, 35, 186

Lost Dutchman Mine, 133

McDonald's, first drive-thru, 19

Murray Springs Clovis Site, 42

NASA, 25, 65

Navajo Code Talkers, 41

O.K. Corral, 50

Oraibi, 28

Poker game, longest, 15

Pleasant Valley War, 48

Pluto, discovery of, 25

Rodeos, 16

Saloons, 15, 49, 75, 78, 120, 165

Titan Missile Museum, 155

UFOs, Phoenix Lights, 82

Warren Ballpark, 87

Women's suffrage, 88

World War II, 16, 32, 41, 114, 115, 156, 157

MAN-MADE ATTRACTIONS

Anthem Veterans Memorial, 182

Arcosanti, 136

Ashfork-Bainbridge Dam, 118

Astrogeology Science Center, 65

Biosphere 2 (University of Arizona), 69

Bird Cage Theatre, 15

Casa Grande Neon Sign Park, 190

Castle Dome Mine Museum, 175

Coronado Trail National Scenic Byway, 168

Cosanti, 136

Dwarf Car Museum, 158

El Tiradito Wishing Shrine, 5

Four Corners Monument, 59

Glen Canyon Dam, 95

Hall of Flame Museum of Firefighting, 183

Heard Museum, 134

Hoover Dam, 95, 140, 181

Hull Mine, 175

Kalusa Collection (Embry-Riddle Aeronautical University), 157

Kitt Peak National Observatory, 80

Largest desert tortoise, 92

Largest kachina doll, 93

Largest kokopelli, 91

Largest sundial, 93

Largest Wurlitzer pipe organ, 192

London Bridge, 35, 77, 186

Lowell Observatory, 25, 67

Mike O'Callaghan–Pat Tillman Memorial Bridge, 181

Musical Instrument Museum, 194

Navajo Code Talker Memorial, 41

O.K. Corral, 50

Parker Dam, 30, 31

Rattlesnake Bridge, 159

Sharlot Hall Museum, 130

Skydive Arizona, 169

SkyVenture Arizona, 169

Standin' on a Corner Park, 115

Taliesin West, 135

Whiskey Row, 75, 94

Yuma Territorial Prison State Park, 23, 78, 112, 113

MISCELLANEOUS

5 C's, 117

Altitude/elevation, 1, 7, 9, 17, 21, 24, 25, 37, 38, 45, 66, 72, 97, 98, 100, 101, 105, 141, 142, 168, 198

Arizona Cardinals, 85, 181

Arizona counties, 26

Arizona flag, 44

Baseball, 86, 87

Bigfoot/Mogollon Monster, 18

Bola tie, 56

Hiking, 22, 24, 29, 40, 47, 62, 68, 79,

84, 89, 116, 118, 142, 143, 145, 170, 175, 178, 196
Interstate 19, 96
Largest petrified tree, 90
Life zones, 66, 97, 98
Make-A-Wish Foundation, 70
Mining, 15, 33, 36, 64, 72, 73, 75, 117, 120, 133, 138, 161, 168, 174, 175, 180, 199
Monsoons, 10, 102, 103, 124
Movies and television, 104, 105, 125, 199
Salt deposits, 161
Sunsets, 107, 178, Bonus Fact
Volcanoes, 6, 24, 47, 65, 89, 133, 160
Temperature, 34, 37, 38, 66, 98, 102, 142
Wide-open spaces, 106
Wurlitzer pipe organ, 192

NATIVE AMERICANS

American Indian Veterans National Memorial, 134
Ancestral Puebloans, 27
Apache, 20, 22, 26, 27, 133
Arizona counties, 26
Arizona Tribes, 20
Artwork, 134, 171
Casa Grande Ruins National Monument, 6, 109
Clovis culture, 42
Grand Falls/Mooney Falls, 29
Havasupai 12, 20, 29
Heard Museum, 134
Hohokam people, 6, 46, 109
Hopi, 20, 27, 28
Native American lands, 20
Native Seeds/SEARCH, 197
Navajo Code Talkers, 41
Navajo Nation, 20, 58, 59, 60, 191
Navajo Nation Zoo, 191
Oraibi, 28
Tohono O'odham, 20, 55, 80
Ute, 59
Zunis, 20, 27

PEOPLE

Adams, Ernie, 158
Armstrong, Allen, 175
Armstrong, Stephanie, 175
Bainbridge, Francis, 118
Banks, Ernie, 86
Barnes, Pancho, 119
Bautista de Anza, Juan, 153
Barrett, James, 47
Beale, Edward Fitzgerald, 116
Berlin, Irving, 188
Billy the Kid, 49, 56
Blevins, Andy, 48
Bonaparte, Napoleon, 35

Bradbury, Ray, 151

Brady, Diamond Jim, 15

Brewster, David, 122

Browne, Jackson, 115

Buchanan, James, 116

Busch, Adolph, 15

Bush, Nellie T., 31

Cahill, Frank "Windy," 49

Carraro, Alessio, 187

Carroll, Lewis, 132

Claiborne, Billy, 50

Clanton, Billy, 50

Clanton, Ike, 50

Clark, Marion, 163

Clark, Russell "Art," 111

Cochise, 26

Colter, Mary Elizabeth Jane, 137, 145

Cooley, Corydon, 163

Coolidge, Calvin, 130

Contreras, Daniel, 149

Cortés, Hernán, 123

Delgadillo, Angel, 32

Delgadillo, Juan, 32

DeMille, Cecil B., 105

Dickens, Charles, 35

Dillinger, John, 111

Doby, Larry, 86

Donovan, Simon, 159

Douglass, Andrew Ellicott, 67

Duppa, Phillip Darrell, 46

Earhart, Amelia, 119

Earp, Morgan, 50

Earp, Virgil, 50

Earp, Wyatt, 50

Evans, William, 78

Flake, William Jordan, 164

Flin, Jules, 147

Flin, Monica, 147, 148

Frey, Glenn, 115

Gable, Clark, 188

Gage, Dennis, 158

Garrett, Pat, 49

Gowan, David, 22

Graham, Tom, 48

Greenlee, Mason, 26

Greicius, Christopher James, 70

Gulley, Boyce Luther, 187

Gulley, Mary Lou, 187

Hall, Sharlot Madbrith, 130

Harlow, Jean, 185

Harrison, Benjamin, 109

Hart, Pearl, 112

Hayes, Rutherford B., 150

Hearst, George Randolph, 15

Holliday, Doc, 15, 50

Horn, Tom, 48

Houck, Chet, 78

Hunt, George Wylie Paul, 193

Ives, Joseph Christmas, 140

Jack the Ripper, 35

Johnson, Woody, 148

Kalusa, John W., 157

Kolb, Ellsworth, 141

Kolb, Emery, 141

Leatherwood, R.N. "Bob," 150

Leslie, Buckskin Frank, 112

Lightfoot, Gordon, 184

Lowell, Percival, 25, 67

Mack, Connie, 87

Makley, Charles, 111

Martin, Billy, 87

Masterson, Bat, 15

Maytag, Robert, 13

McAllister, Frances, 198

McCulloch, Robert P., 35, 186

McGraw, John, 87

McKee, Eddie, 84

McLaury, Frank, 50

McLaury, Tom, 50

Merriam, Clinton Hart, 66

Michelangelo, 123

Mix, Tom, 185

Moeur, Benjamin, 31

Mogollon, Juan Ignacio Flores, 17

Monroe, Marilyn, 188

Nightingale, Florence, 35

Nephew, Rufus a.k.a. Climax Jim, 23

O'Callaghan, Mike, 181

Oliveras, Juan, 5

Ott, Mel, 87

Owens, Commodore Perry, 48

Peck, Walter, 63

Pemberton, Pete, 78

Phipps, Johnny, 165

Pierpont, Harry, 111

Pope Leo XIII, 150

Purcell, Roy, 180

Queen Victoria, 35

Rigney, Walt, 165

Rogers, Will, 119

Roosevelt, Eleanor, 119

Roosevelt, Theodore, 89, 130

Ross, Betsy, 123

Russell, Kurt, 82

Ruth, Adolph, 133

Schmaltz, Daren, 158

Shatner, William, 125

Shaw, John, 78

Shewalter, Dale, 170

Sinatra, Frank, 188

Snow, Erastus, 164

Soleri, Paolo, 136

Speaker, Tris, 87

Spicer, Wells, 50

Stevens, I. W., 18

Sulit, Gene, 188

Swilling, John W. "Jack," 46, 47

Sykes, Godfrey, 132

Symington, Fife, 82

Tewksbury, Ed, 48

Tillman, Pat, 181

Tombaugh, Clyde, 25

Tovrea, Della, 187

Tovrea, E. A., 187

Vasquez de Coronado, Francisco, 168

Veeck, Bill, 86

Wagner, Honus, 87

Waltz, Jacob, 133

Warner, Ben, 185

Webb, Del, 131

Wilson, Woodrow, 109

Wong, Joe, 93

Wright, Frank Lloyd, 135, 136, 188

Yellot, John, 93

PHOENIX (VALLEY OF THE SUN)

Arizona Biltmore, 188

Arizona Cowboy College, 166

Bat cave, 107

Black sphinx dates, 177

Camp Papago Park, 114

Carefree, 93, 167, 184

Carefree Highway, 184

Chandler, 200

Cosanti, 136

Desert Botanical Garden, 132

Fountain Hills, 81, 186

Gilbert, 189, 190

Hall of Flame Museum of Fire-fighting, 183

Heard Museum, 134

Hiking, 195, 196

Largest kachina doll, 93

Largest sundial, 93

Macayo's, 148

Make-A-Wish Foundation, 70

McDowell Sonoran Preserve, 195

Mesa, 192

Musical Instrument Museum, 194

Mystery Castle, 187

Organ Stop Pizza, 192

Papago Park, 193

Phoenix history, 46, 86

Phoenix facts, 1, 45, 107, 114, 134, 195

Phoenix Lights, 82

Phoenix Zoo, 13

Salt deposits, 161

Salt River, 40, 46, 161

Scottsdale, 135, 144, 166, 195

South Mountain Park, 187, 195

Sunshine, 1

Surprise, 167

Taliesin West, 135

Tempe, 48, 195

Tovrea Castle at Carraro Heights, 187

Tumbleweed Christmas tree, 200

Wildflowers, 52

PLANTS

Boojum tree, 132

Cactus, 10, 14, 53, 54, 55, 123, 130, 168, 178, 187, 195

Cottonwood tree, largest, 39
 Creosote, 103
Date palms, 1, 176, 177
Ponderosa pines, 7, 8, 17, 66, 67,
 165, 171, 198
Organ pipe cactus, 178
Rosebush, largest, 51
Russian thistle, 200
Saguaro, 6, 10, 14, 20, 52, 53, 54, 55,
 98, 102, 103, 129, 144, 149, 178, 184
Spruce-fir forest, 101
Tumbleweed, 200
Wildflowers, 47, 52, 53, 54, 55, 198

ROUTE 66

Arizona saved Route 66, 32
Beale Wagon Road, 116
Burma-Shave signs, 64
Grand Canyon Caverns, 63, 64
Giganticus Headicus, 64
Hackberry General Store, 64
Longest stretch of Route 66, 64
Neon, 190
Oatman burros, 33, 64
Petrified Forest National Park, 81, 89
Powerhouse Visitor Center, 64, 179
Route 66 Electric Vehicle Museum,
 179
Route 66 Museum, 64
Standin' on a Corner Park, 115

TOWNS

Ajo, 117, 178
Alpine, 168
Anthem, 182
Ash Fork, 64, 118
Bagdad, 117, 167
Bisbee, 72, 73, 75, 76, 87, 117, 138, 174
Bullhead City, 92
Bumble Bee, 167
Camp Verde, 81, 91, 125
Casa Grande, 190
Chloride, 167, 180
Clarkdale, 199
Clifton, 168
Coolidge, 109
Cordes Junction, 136
Cottonwood, 81
Douglas, 119, 154
Eagar, 168
Eloy, 169
Flagstaff, 7, 24, 25, 65, 66, 67, 81, 94,
 105, 160, 170, 171, 198
Gila Bend, 82, 173
Globe, 23, 48, 117, 193
Green Valley, 96
Hackberry, 64
Holbrook, 48, 75, 89, 90, 144
Jerome, 117, 120, 121, 122, 199
Kingman, 64, 161, 179, 180
Lake Havasu City, 34, 35, 71, 77

Maricopa, 158
Miami, 117
Morenci, 117, 168
Nogales, 74, 96
Nothing, 167
Oatman, 33, 36, 64
Oracle, 69, 81
Page, 60, 79
Parker, 30, 31
Payson, 16, 22
Peach Springs, 64
Pima, 100
Pine, 22
Pinetop, 165
Prescott, 16, 45, 75, 94, 130, 157, 185
Ray, 117
Rio Rico, 96
Rock Springs, 185
Safford, 98, 100, 117, 152
Sahuarita, 96, 155
Sedona, 81, 171, 172, 199
Seligman, 32, 63, 64
Show Low, 163
Sierra Vista, 19, 42, 127
Skull Valley, 39, 167
Snowflake, 164
Solomonville, 23
Springerville, 23, 168
St. David, 152
St. Johns, 23
Teec Nos Pos, 59

Thatcher, 100
Tombstone, 15, 50, 51, 117, 167
Topock, 64
Top-of-the-World, 167
Tuba City, 167
Truxton, 64
Tubac, 96, 153
Why, 167
Wickenburg, 46, 110, 167, 184
Wikieup, 167
Williams, 7, 75, 190
Window Rock, 41, 58, 191
Winslow, 11, 23, 29, 78, 115, 137
Young, 48
Yuma, 1, 4, 21, 23, 38, 47, 78, 94, 112, 113, 175, 176, 177

TUCSON

Aircraft boneyard, 156
Bradbury, Ray, 151
Civil War, 47
Desert Laboratory, 132
Dillinger, John, 111
Douglass, Andrew Ellicott, 67
El Charro Café, 147, 148
El Tiradito Wishing Shrine, 5
Hotel Congress, 111
Interstate 19, 96
Kitt Peak National Observatory, 80
La Fiesta de los Vaqueros, 16

Laboratory of Tree Ring Research, 67

Mount Lemmon, 98, 99

Native Seeds/SEARCH, 197

Neon, 190

New Year's Eve, 94

Old Pueblo, 150

Pima Air and Space Museum, 156

Rattlesnake Bridge, 159

Saguaro National Park, 6, 178

Sky Island Parkway, 98

Sonoran hot dog, 149

Steward Observatory, 67

Sunshine, 1

Territorial capital, 45

Titan Missile Museum, 155

UNESCO City of Gastronomy, 146

University of Arizona's Biosphere 2, 69

University of Arizona Campus Krutch Garden, 132

Wildflowers, 52

WILDLIFE / ANIMALS

Arabian oryx, 13

Bats, 54, 107, 108

Beavers, 199

Bighorn sheep, 152

Bird species, 97, 127, 128, 152

Black bears, 101

Brown vine snake, 97

Burros, 33, 64

Butterflies, 54, 162

California condors, 128

Camels, 42, 116

Cochineal, 123

Coyotes, 199

Eagles, 191, 199

Elegant trogons, 97, 128

Gila monster, 43, 126

Hawks, 199

Herons, 199

Hummingbirds, 127

Jaguars, 3, 97

Javelinas, 199

Keepers of the Wild, 64

Mexican gray wolves, 83, 168

Mount Graham red squirrels, 101

Mule deer, 199

Mules, 12, 141, 145

Navajo Nation Zoo, 191

Ocelots, 3, 97

Phoenix Zoo, 13

Rattlesnakes, 84, 126, 129, 139, 159

Roadrunners, 129

Rock squirrels, 139

Salt River wild horses, 40

Scorpions, 57

Sonoran tiger salamander, 97

Tarantula hawks, 124

Tarantulas, 124, 125

About the Author

ROGER NAYLOR is an award-winning Arizona travel writer and author. He specializes in state and national parks, lonely hiking trails, twisting back roads, diners with burgers sizzling on the grill, small towns, ghost towns, and pie. In 2018, he was inducted into the Arizona Tourism Hall of Fame. His book, *Arizona State Parks*, won the prestigious 2020 New Mexico-Arizona Book Award for Arizona Travel. He repeated the feat when his next one, *Arizona's Scenic Roads and Hikes*, won the 2021 New Mexico-Arizona Book Award in the same category. *Arizona's Scenic Roads and Hikes* was also chosen as the overall Best Arizona Book.

Naylor's work appears most weeks in the *Arizona Republic*. He has also written for the *Guardian*, *USA Today*, *Country Magazine*, *Arizona Highways*, and dozens more. He is the author of several books including *The Amazing Kolb Brothers of Grand Canyon*, *Arizona Kicks on Route 66*, and *Crazy for the Heat: Arizona Tales of Ghosts, Gumshoes, and Bigfoot*. For more information, visit www.rogernaylor.com.